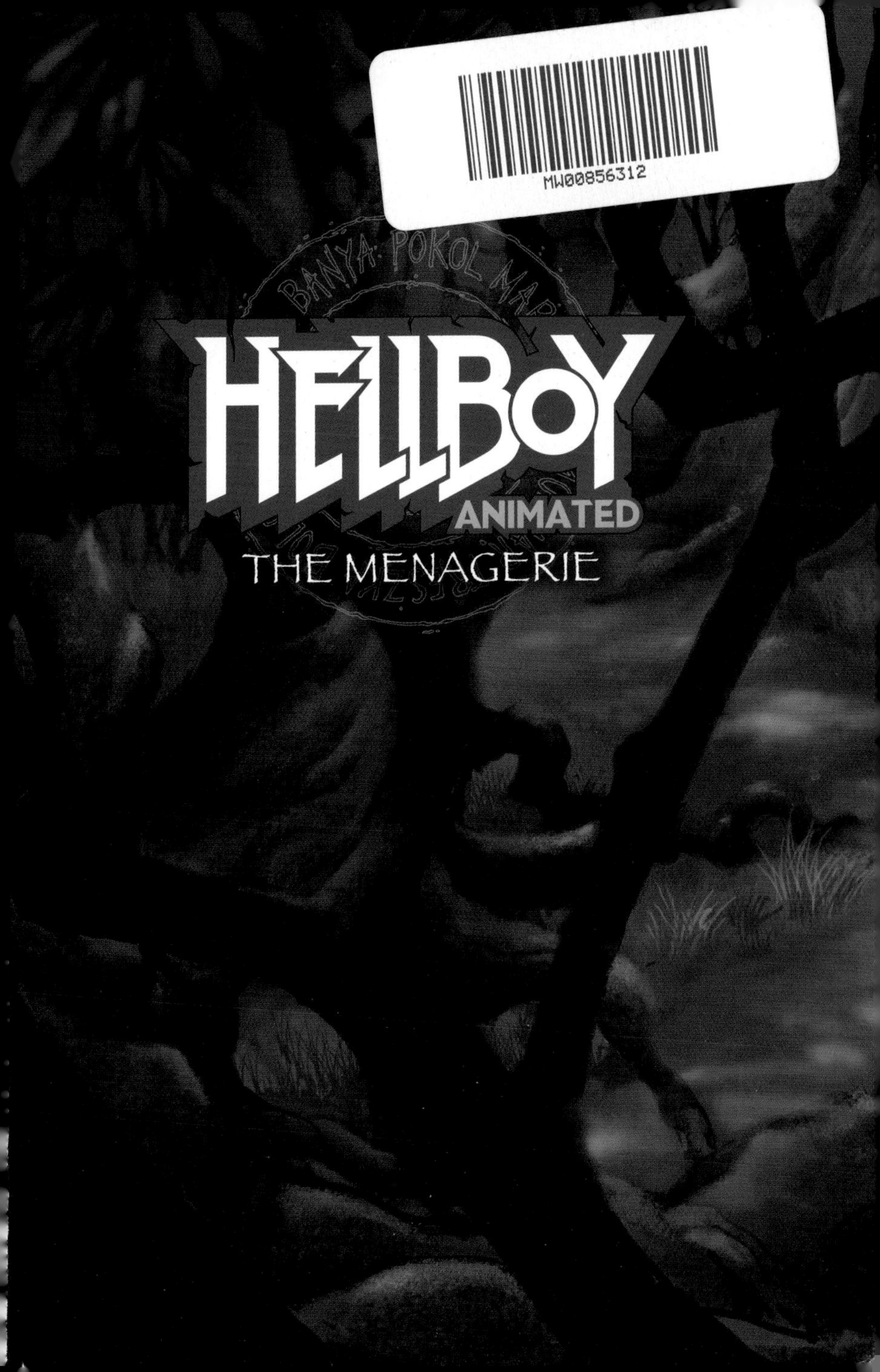
BANYA POKOL MAR
HELLBOY
ANIMATED
THE MENAGERIE

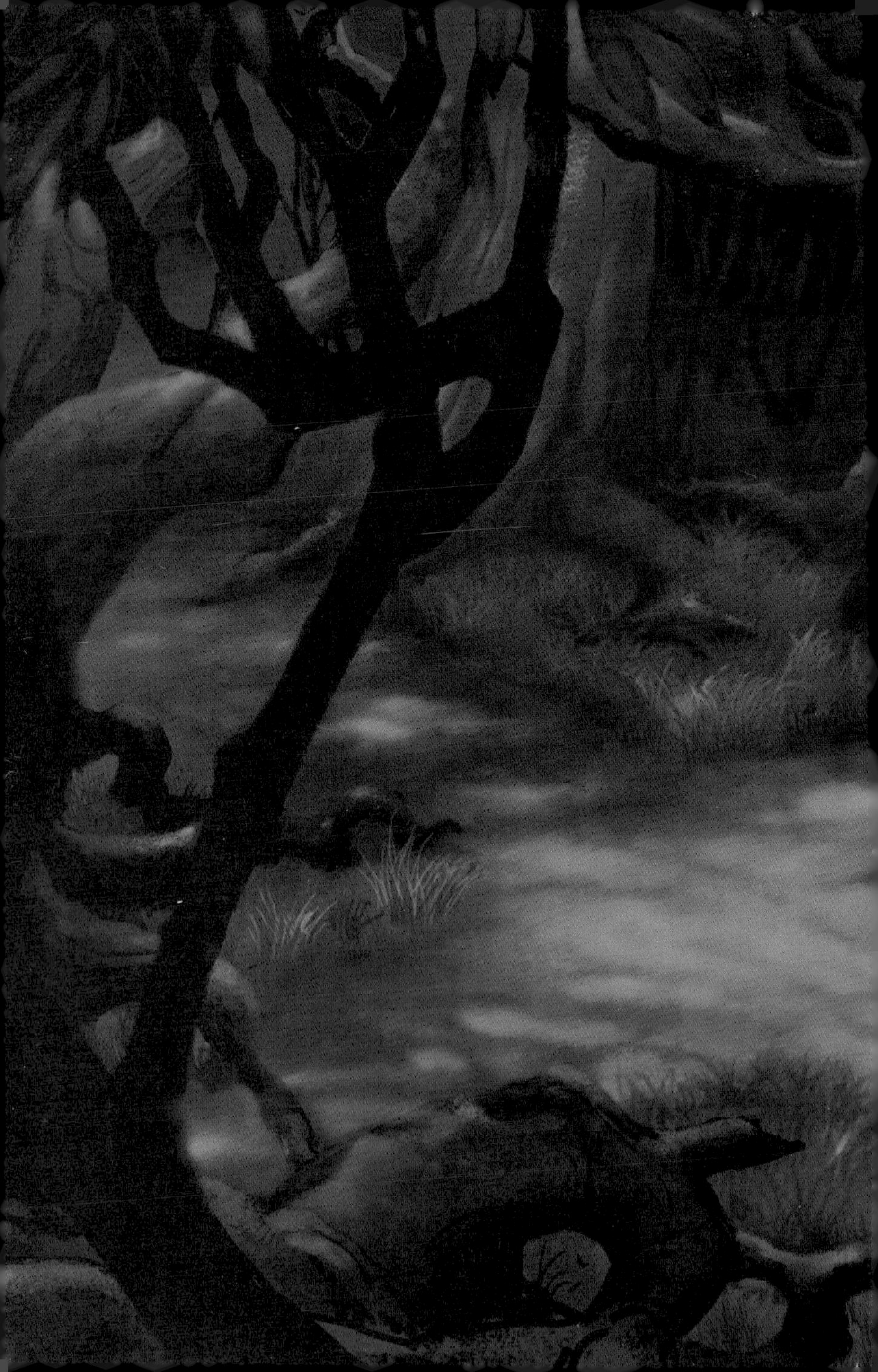

HELLBOY ANIMATED

THE MENAGERIE

Story by JASON HALL

Art by RICK LACY

Colors by MICHELLE MADSEN

Letters by BLAMBOT'S NATE PIEKOS

PINUP

Art by RICK LACY

Colors by MICHELLE MADSEN

SMALL VICTORIES

Art by FABIO LAGUNA

Story and Letters by NATE PIEKOS

Colors by MICHELLE MADSEN

Cover Art by HUMBERTO RAMOS

Cover colors by Leonardo Olea

Hellboy and the B.P.R.D. created by MIKE MIGNOLA

Dark Horse Books®

Publisher MIKE RICHARDSON

Editor MATT DRYER

Assistant Editor RACHEL EDIDIN

Designer KEITH WOOD

Special Thanks to MIKE and CHRISTINE MIGNOLA,
SCOTT ALLIE, DAVE STEWART, GUY DAVIS, JOHN ARCUDI,
TAD STONES, JASON HVAM, and DAN JACKSON

Published by
Dark Horse Books
A division of Dark Horse Comics, Inc.
10956 SE Main Street
Milwaukie, OR 97222

darkhorse.com

To find a comics shop in your area,
call the Comic Shop Locator Service toll-free at 1-888-266-4226

First Edition: November 2007
ISBN-10: 1-59307-861-7
ISBN-13: 978-1-59307-861-4

1 3 5 7 9 10 8 6 4 2

Printed in China

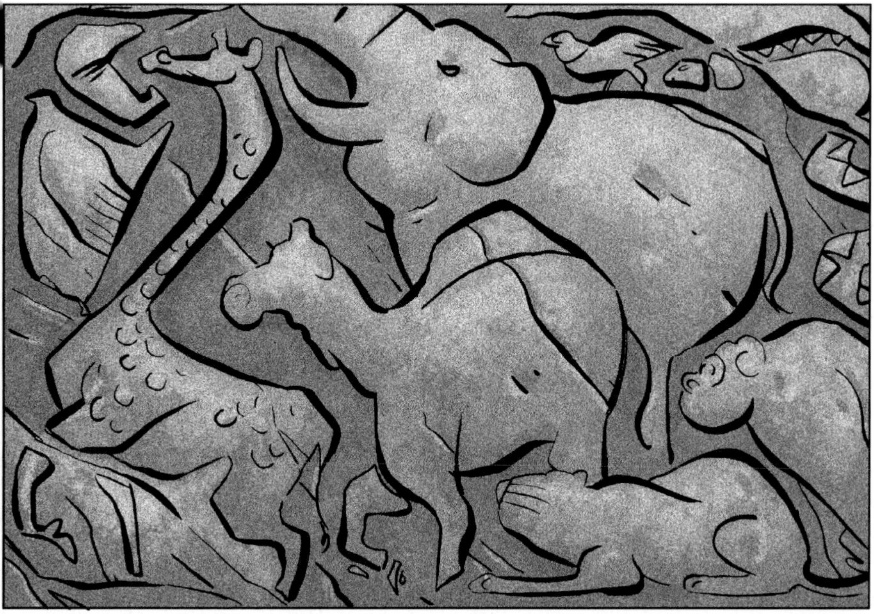

THE MENAGERIE

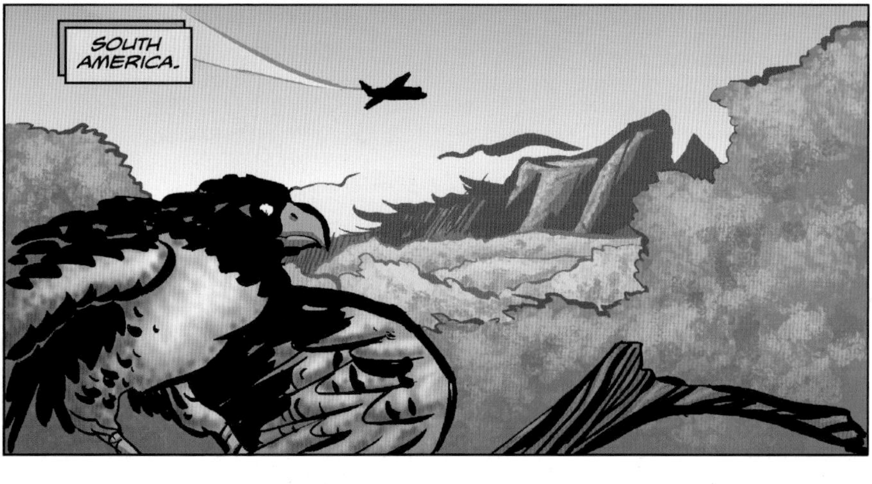
SOUTH AMERICA.

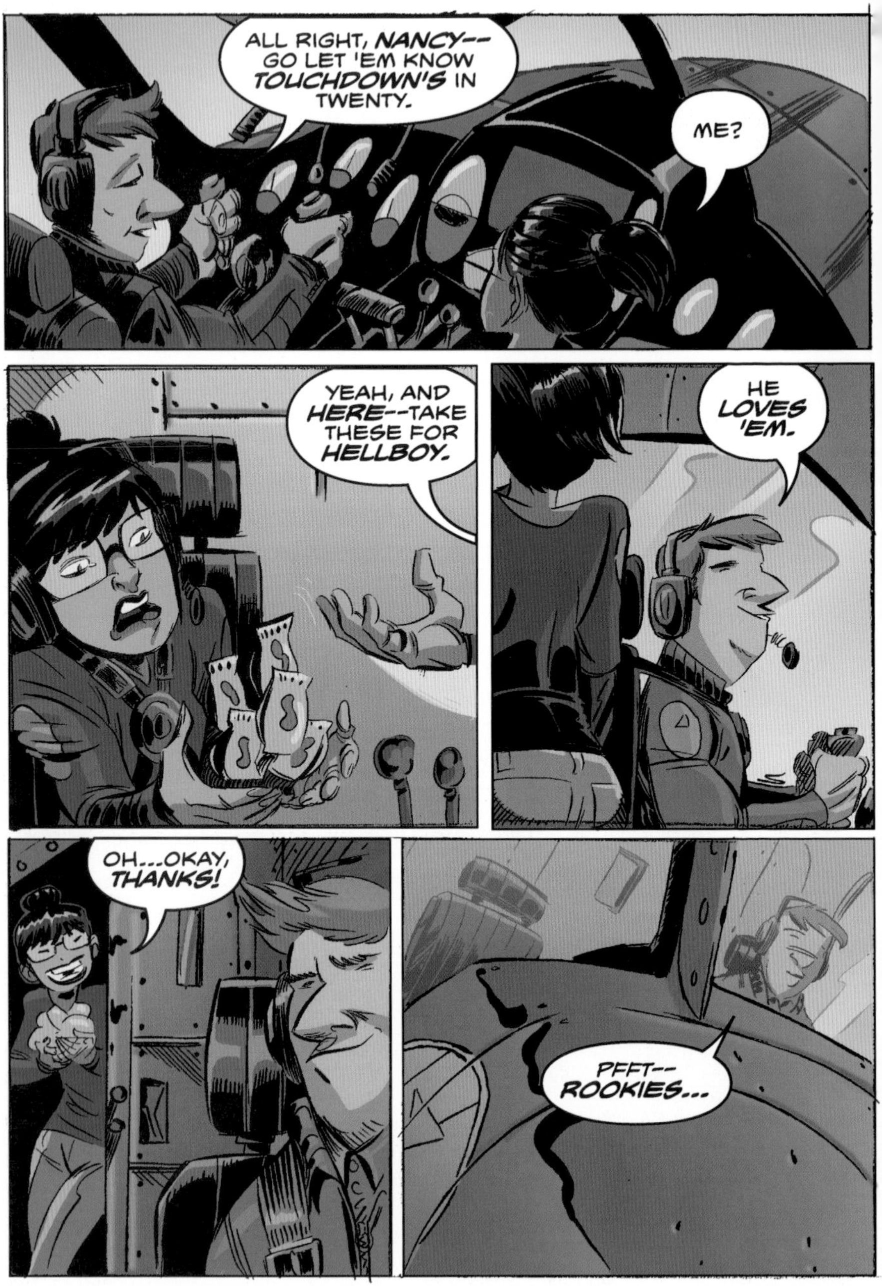
ALL RIGHT, NANCY-- GO LET 'EM KNOW TOUCHDOWN'S IN TWENTY.
ME?
YEAH, AND HERE--TAKE THESE FOR HELLBOY.
HE LOVES 'EM.
OH...OKAY, THANKS!
PFFT-- ROOKIES...

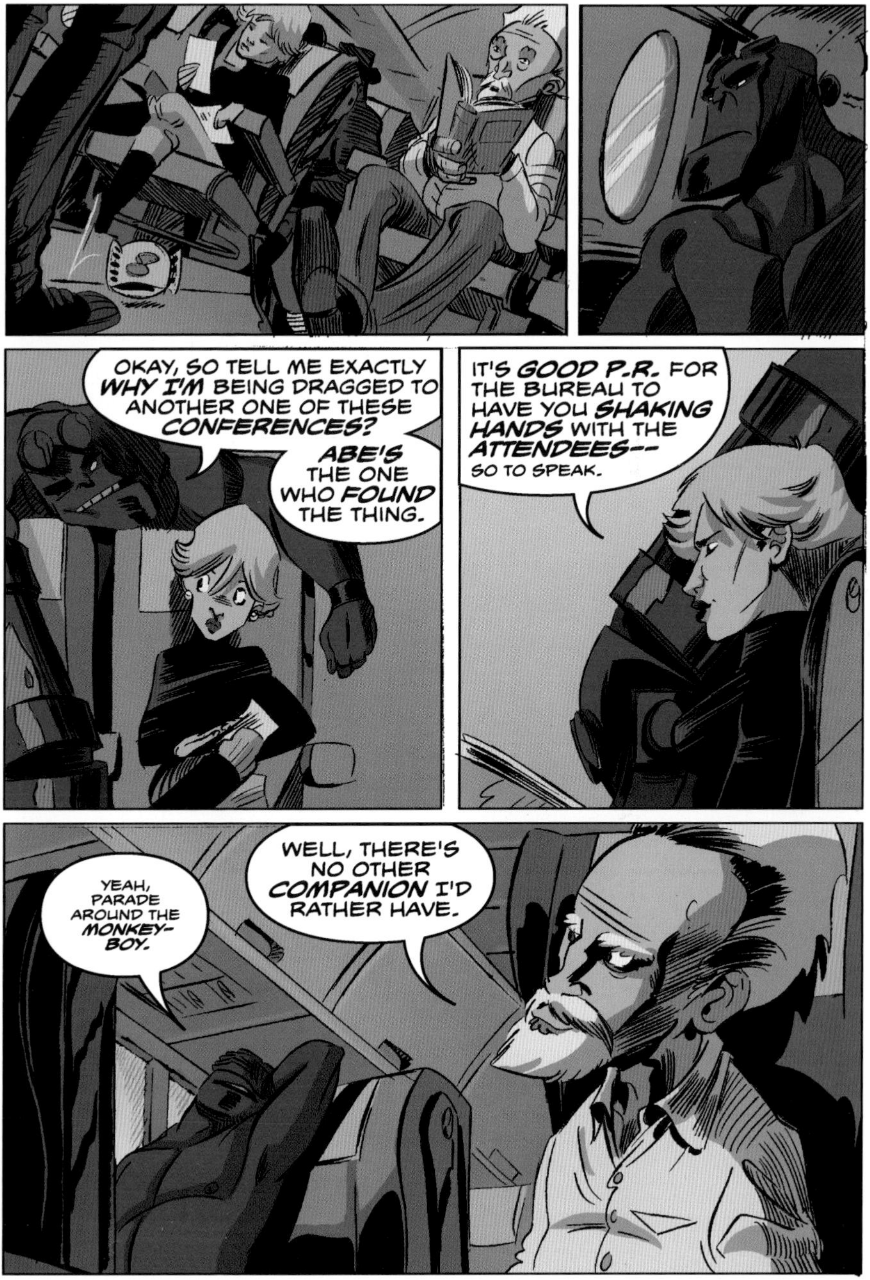
OKAY, SO TELL ME EXACTLY WHY I'M BEING DRAGGED TO ANOTHER ONE OF THESE CONFERENCES?
ABE'S THE ONE WHO FOUND THE THING.
IT'S GOOD P.R. FOR THE BUREAU TO HAVE YOU SHAKING HANDS WITH THE ATTENDEES-- SO TO SPEAK.
WELL, THERE'S NO OTHER COMPANION I'D RATHER HAVE.
YEAH, PARADE AROUND THE MONKEY-BOY.

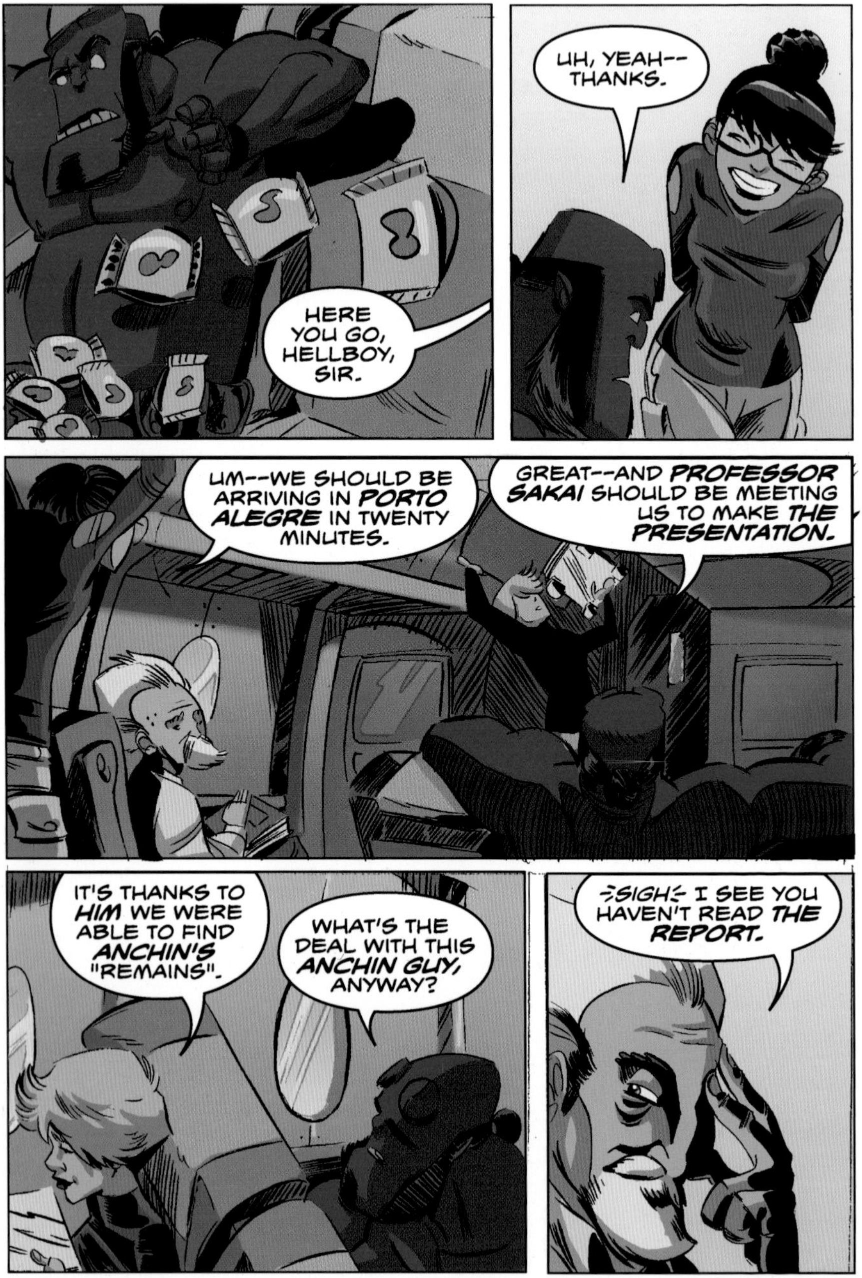
HERE YOU GO, HELLBOY, SIR.
UH, YEAH-- THANKS.
UM--WE SHOULD BE ARRIVING IN PORTO ALEGRE IN TWENTY MINUTES.
GREAT--AND PROFESSOR SAKAI SHOULD BE MEETING US TO MAKE THE PRESENTATION.
IT'S THANKS TO HIM WE WERE ABLE TO FIND ANCHIN'S "REMAINS".
WHAT'S THE DEAL WITH THIS ANCHIN GUY, ANYWAY?
SIGH I SEE YOU HAVEN'T READ THE REPORT.

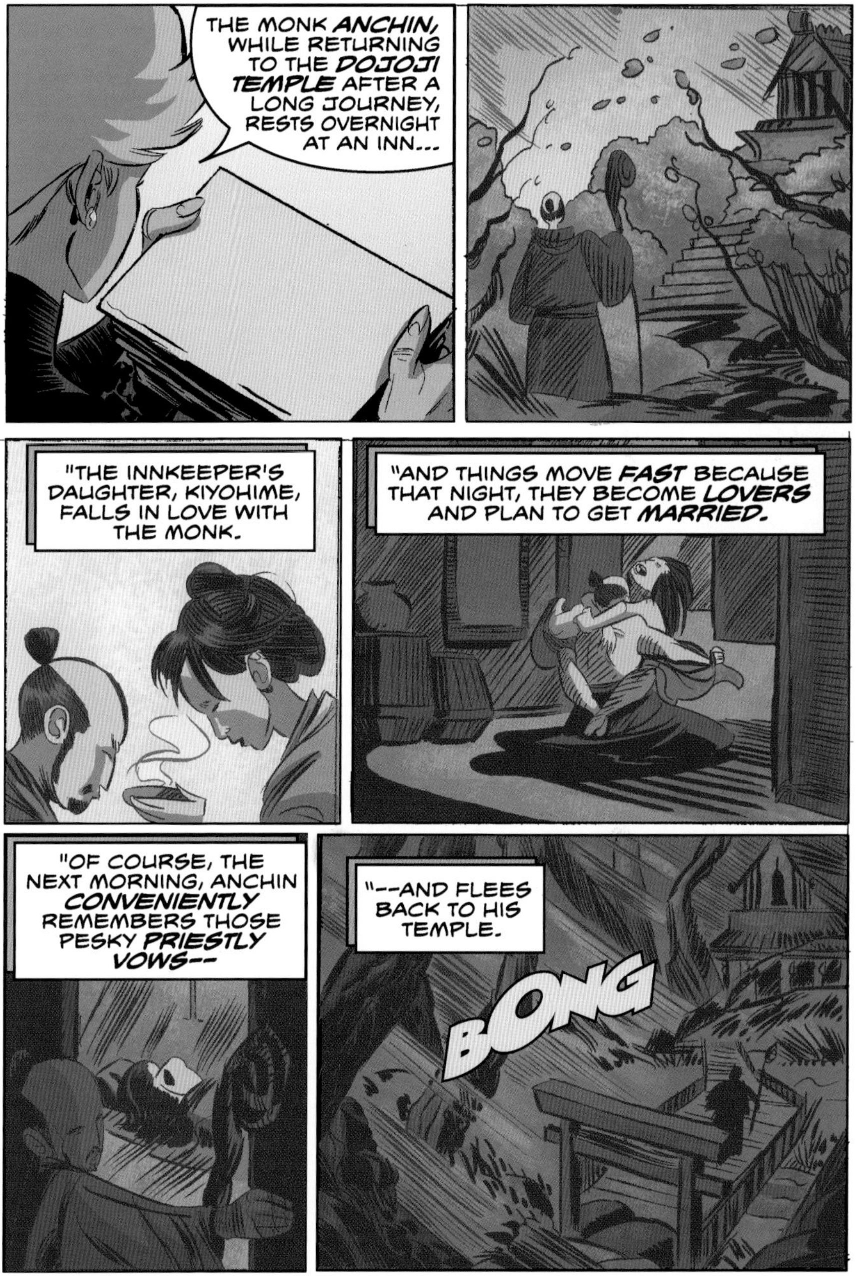
THE MONK ANCHIN, WHILE RETURNING TO THE DOJOJI TEMPLE AFTER A LONG JOURNEY, RESTS OVERNIGHT AT AN INN...
"THE INNKEEPER'S DAUGHTER, KIYOHIME, FALLS IN LOVE WITH THE MONK.
"AND THINGS MOVE FAST BECAUSE THAT NIGHT, THEY BECOME LOVERS AND PLAN TO GET MARRIED.
"OF COURSE, THE NEXT MORNING, ANCHIN CONVENIENTLY REMEMBERS THOSE PESKY PRIESTLY VOWS--
"--AND FLEES BACK TO HIS TEMPLE.
BONG

"KIYOHIME CHASES AFTER HIM--

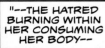

"--THE HATRED BURNING WITHIN HER CONSUMING HER BODY--

"--AND HER VERY SPIRIT--

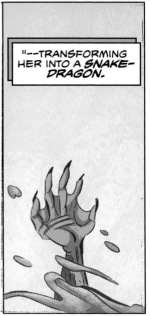

"--TRANSFORMING HER INTO A *SNAKE-DRAGON.*

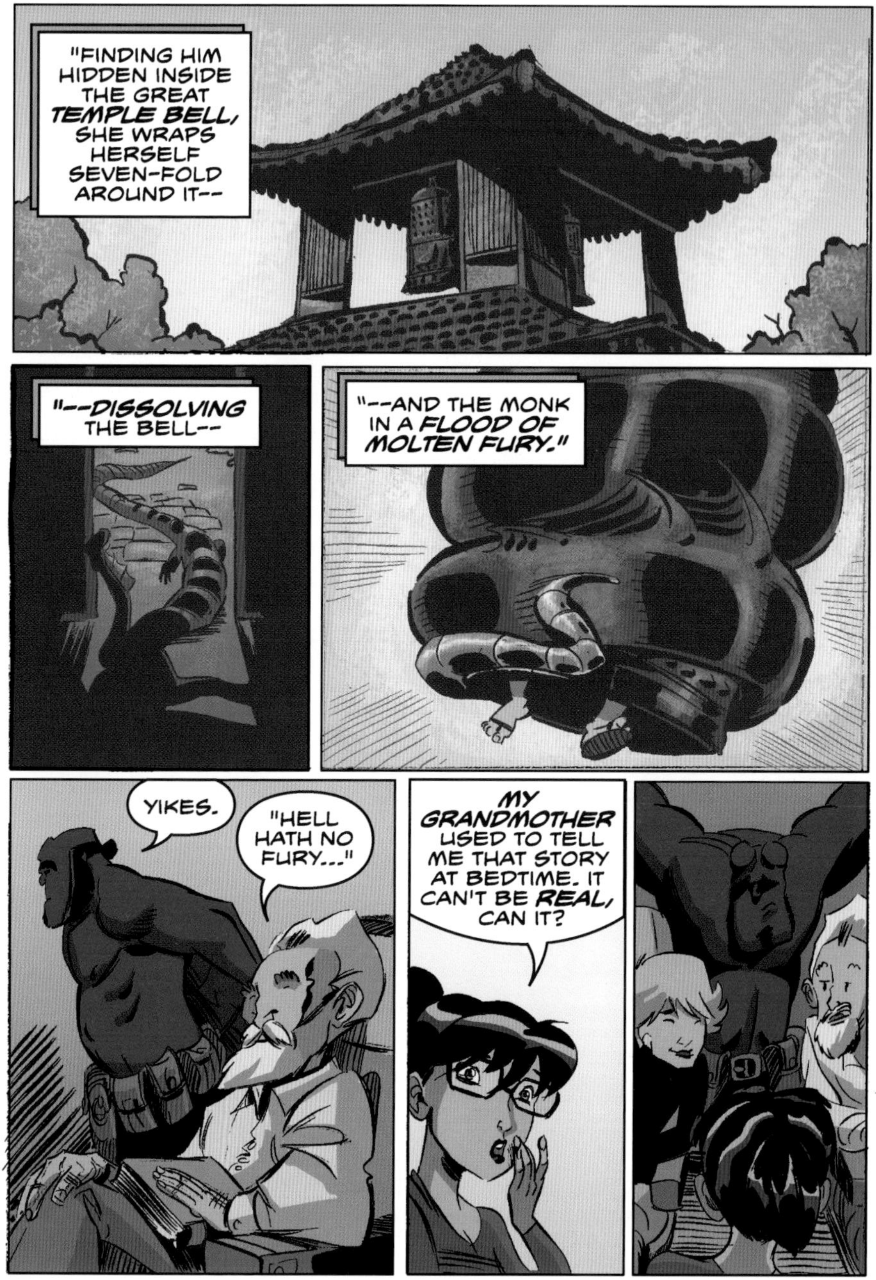
"FINDING HIM HIDDEN INSIDE THE GREAT TEMPLE BELL, SHE WRAPS HERSELF SEVEN-FOLD AROUND IT--
"--DISSOLVING THE BELL--
"--AND THE MONK IN A FLOOD OF MOLTEN FURY."
YIKES.
"HELL HATH NO FURY..."
MY GRANDMOTHER USED TO TELL ME THAT STORY AT BEDTIME. IT CAN'T BE REAL, CAN IT?

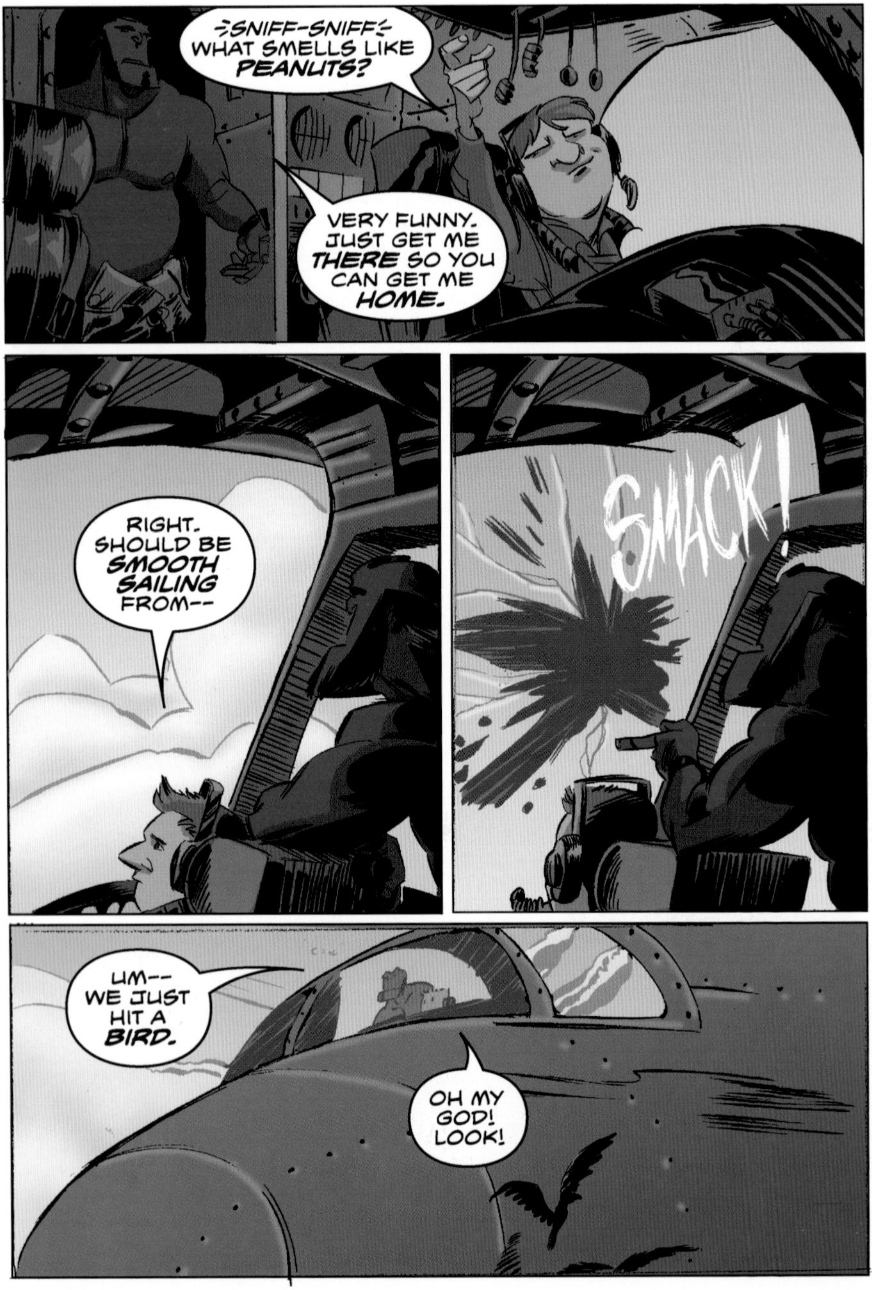

⸗SNIFF-SNIFF⸗ WHAT SMELLS LIKE PEANUTS?
VERY FUNNY. JUST GET ME THERE SO YOU CAN GET ME HOME.
RIGHT. SHOULD BE SMOOTH SAILING FROM--
SMACK!
UM-- WE JUST HIT A BIRD.
OH MY GOD! LOOK!

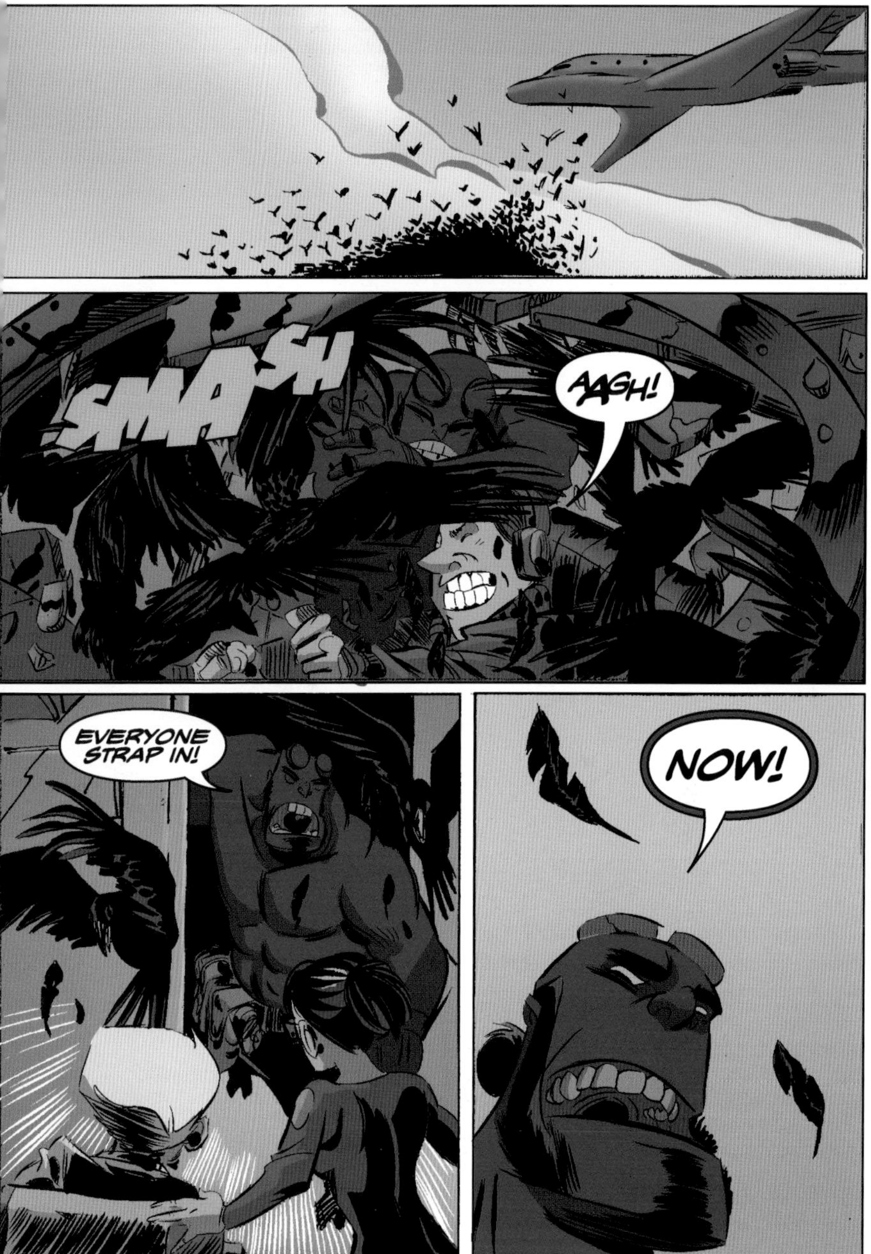
SMASH
AAGH!
EVERYONE STRAP IN!
NOW!

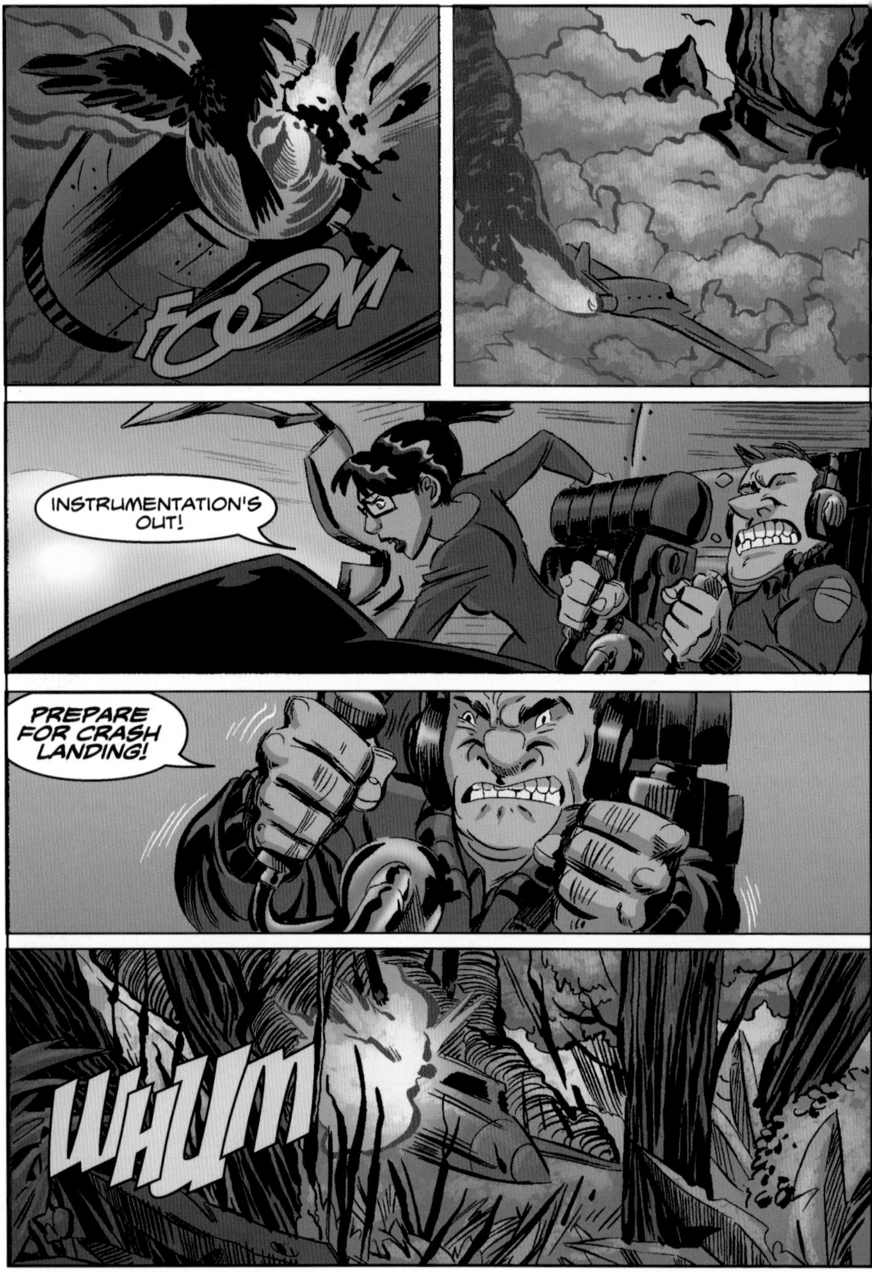
FOOM
INSTRUMENTATION'S OUT!
PREPARE FOR CRASH LANDING!
WHUM

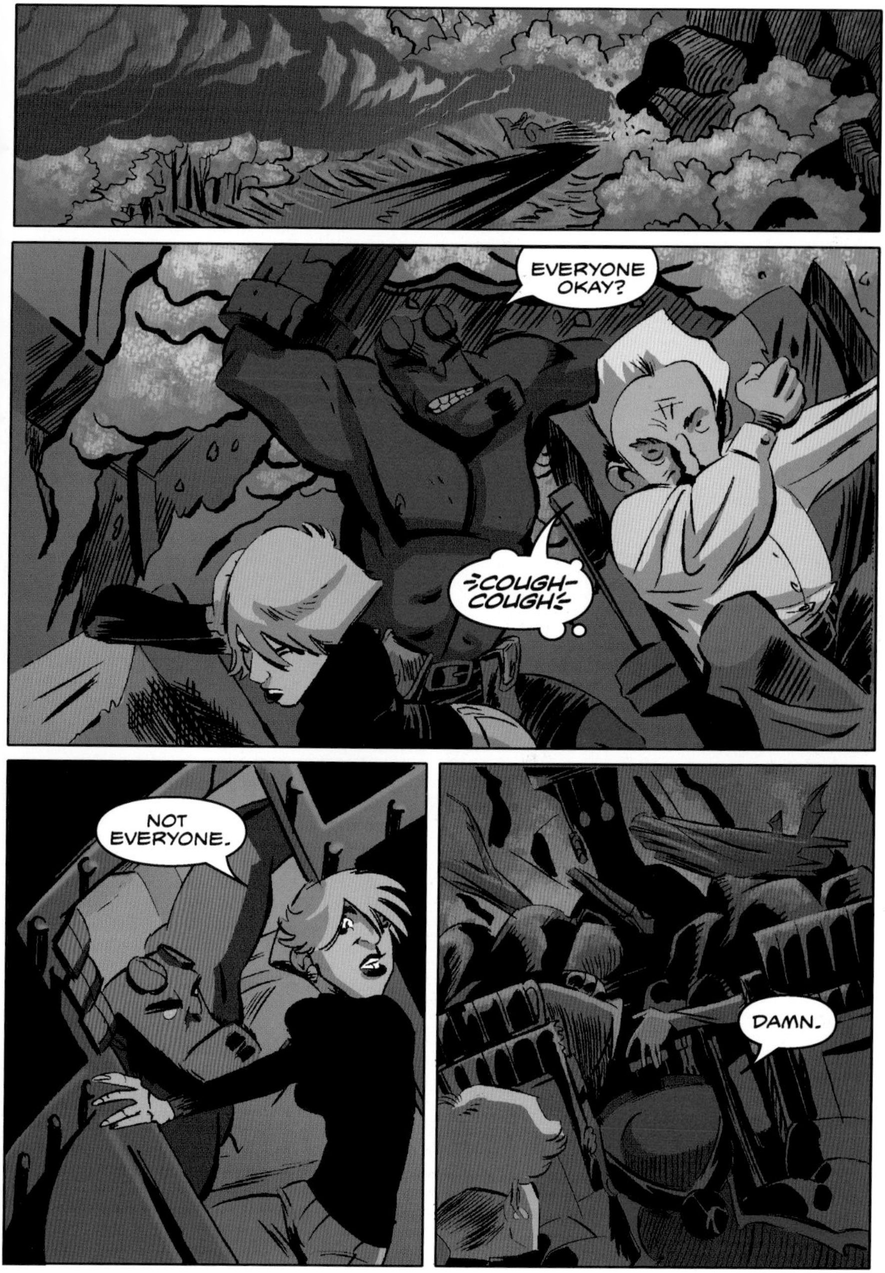
EVERYONE OKAY?
COUGH-COUGH
NOT EVERYONE.
DAMN.

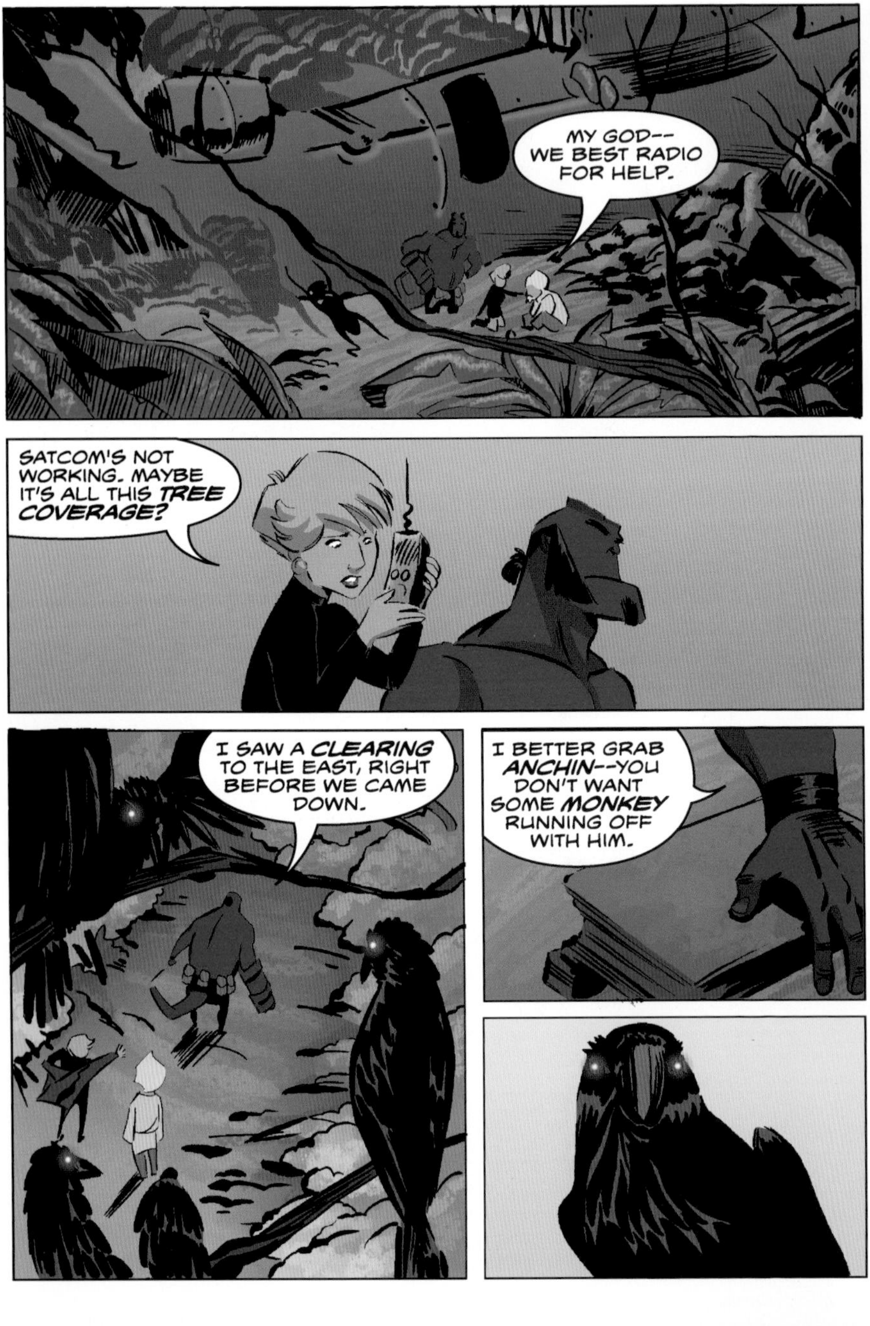
MY GOD--
WE BEST RADIO
FOR HELP.
SATCOM'S NOT
WORKING. MAYBE
IT'S ALL THIS *TREE*
COVERAGE?
I SAW A *CLEARING*
TO THE EAST, RIGHT
BEFORE WE CAME
DOWN.
I BETTER GRAB
ANCHIN--YOU
DON'T WANT
SOME *MONKEY*
RUNNING OFF
WITH HIM.

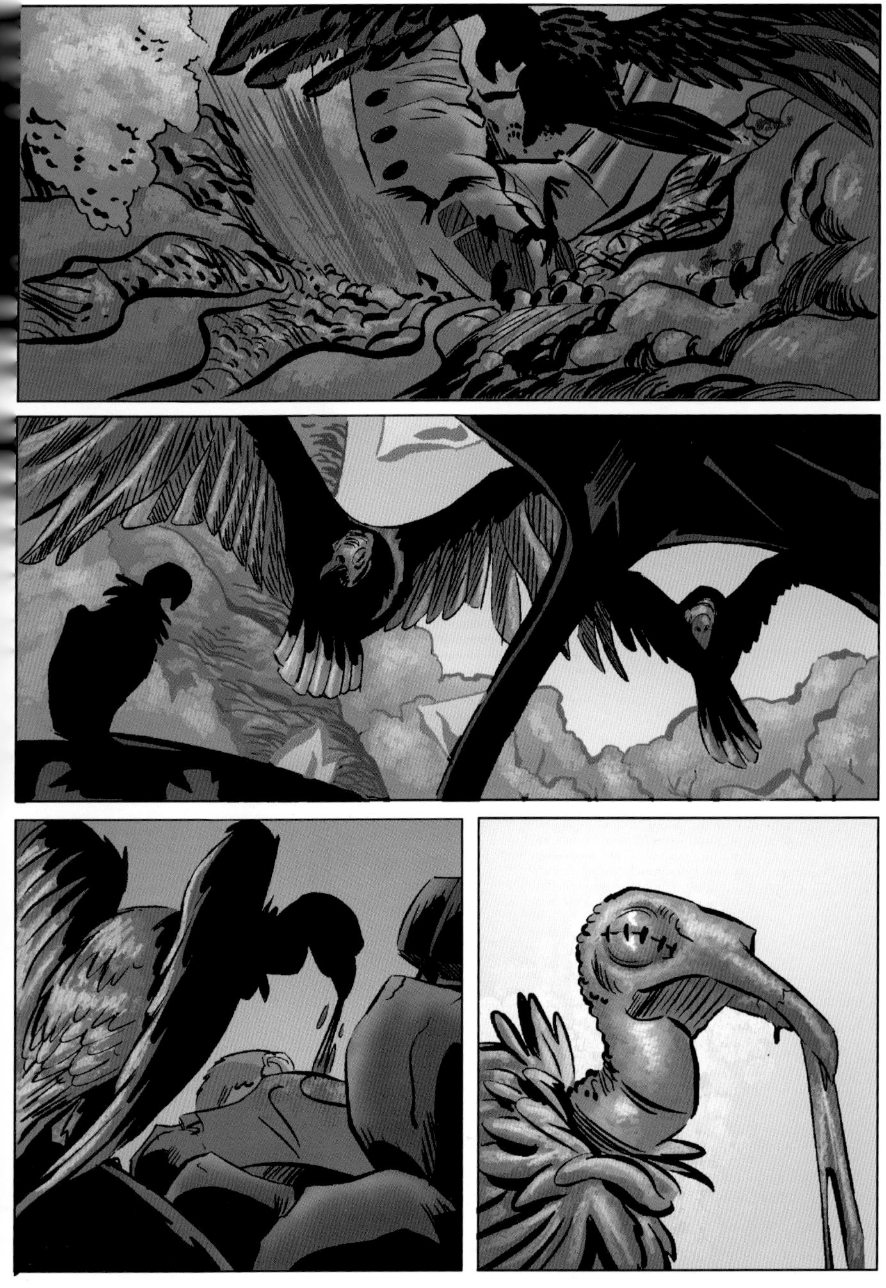

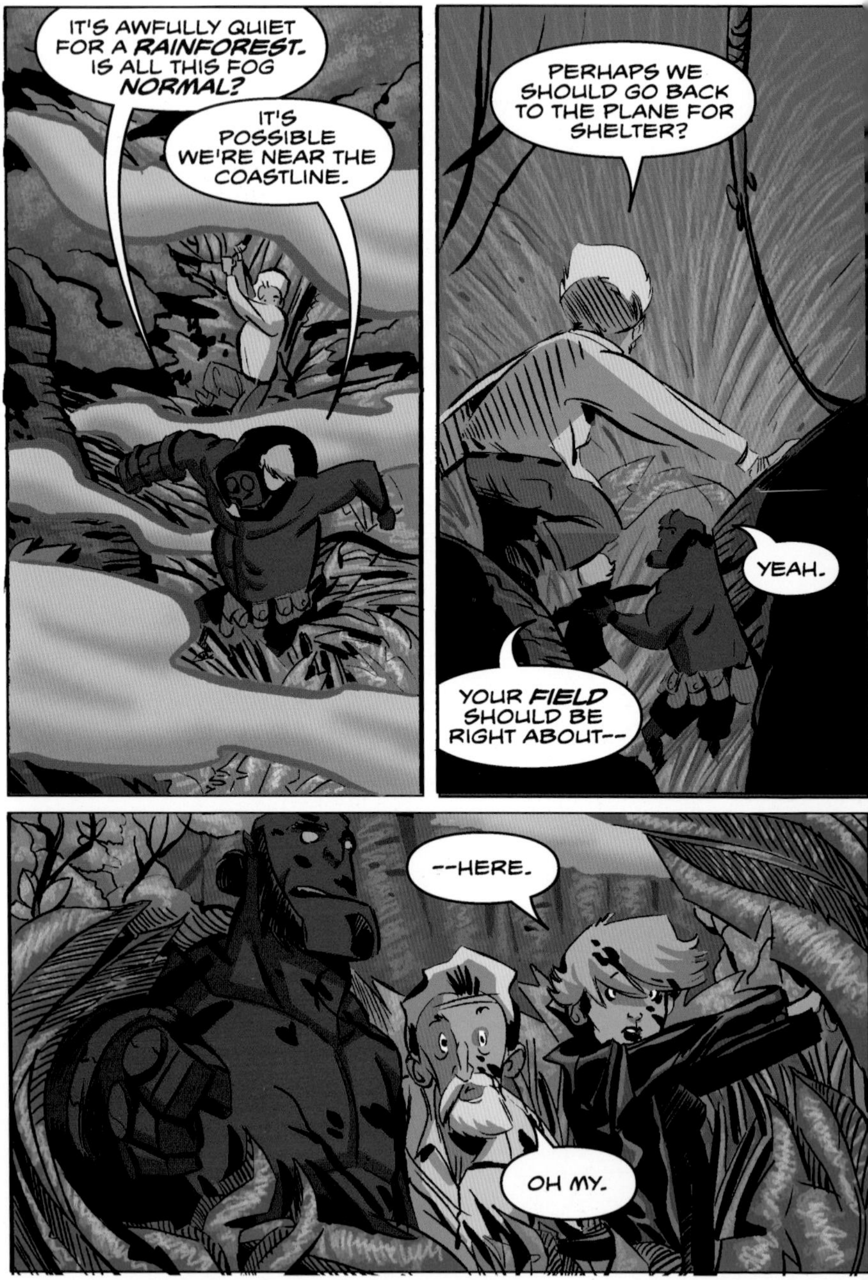
IT'S AWFULLY QUIET FOR A RAINFOREST. IS ALL THIS FOG NORMAL?
IT'S POSSIBLE WE'RE NEAR THE COASTLINE.
PERHAPS WE SHOULD GO BACK TO THE PLANE FOR SHELTER?
YEAH.
YOUR FIELD SHOULD BE RIGHT ABOUT--
--HERE.
OH MY.

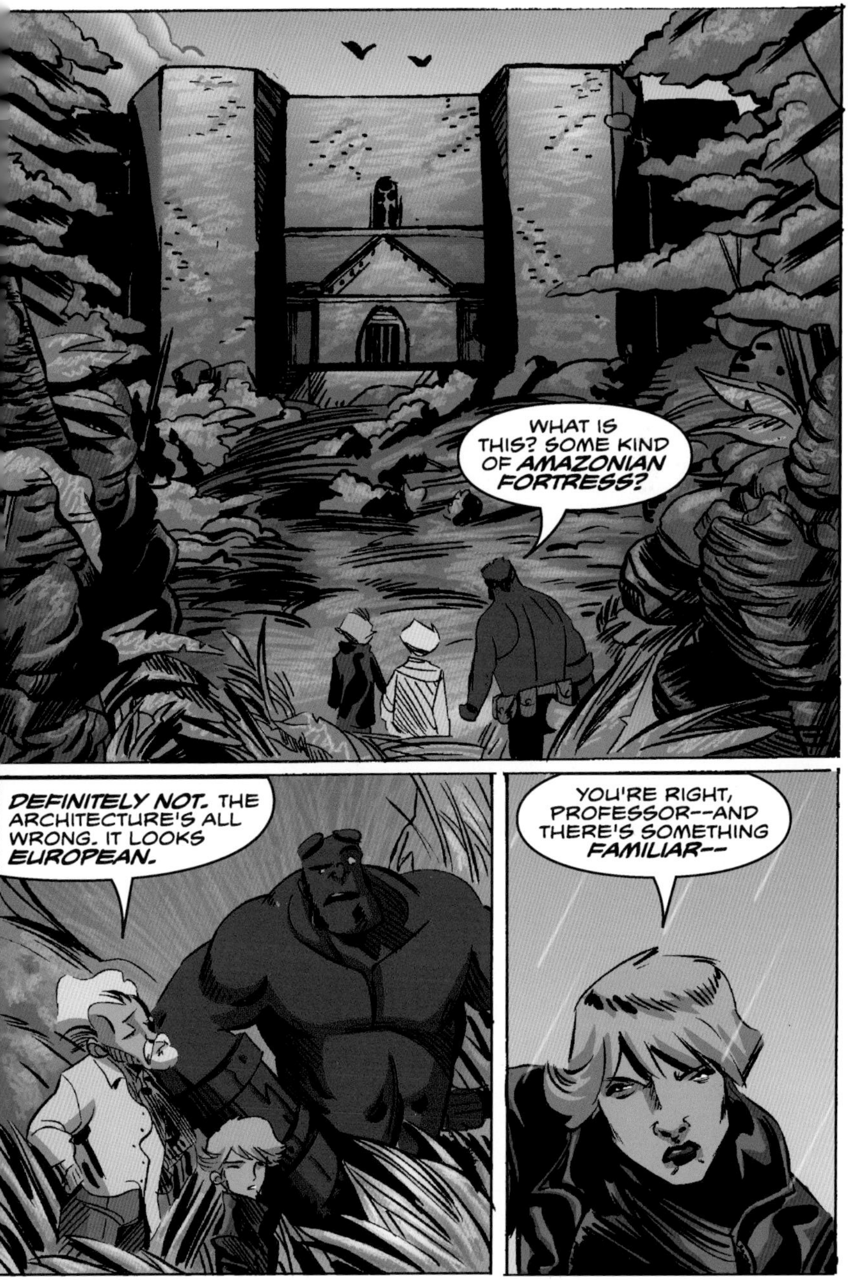
WHAT IS THIS? SOME KIND OF AMAZONIAN FORTRESS?
DEFINITELY NOT. THE ARCHITECTURE'S ALL WRONG. IT LOOKS EUROPEAN.
YOU'RE RIGHT, PROFESSOR--AND THERE'S SOMETHING FAMILIAR--

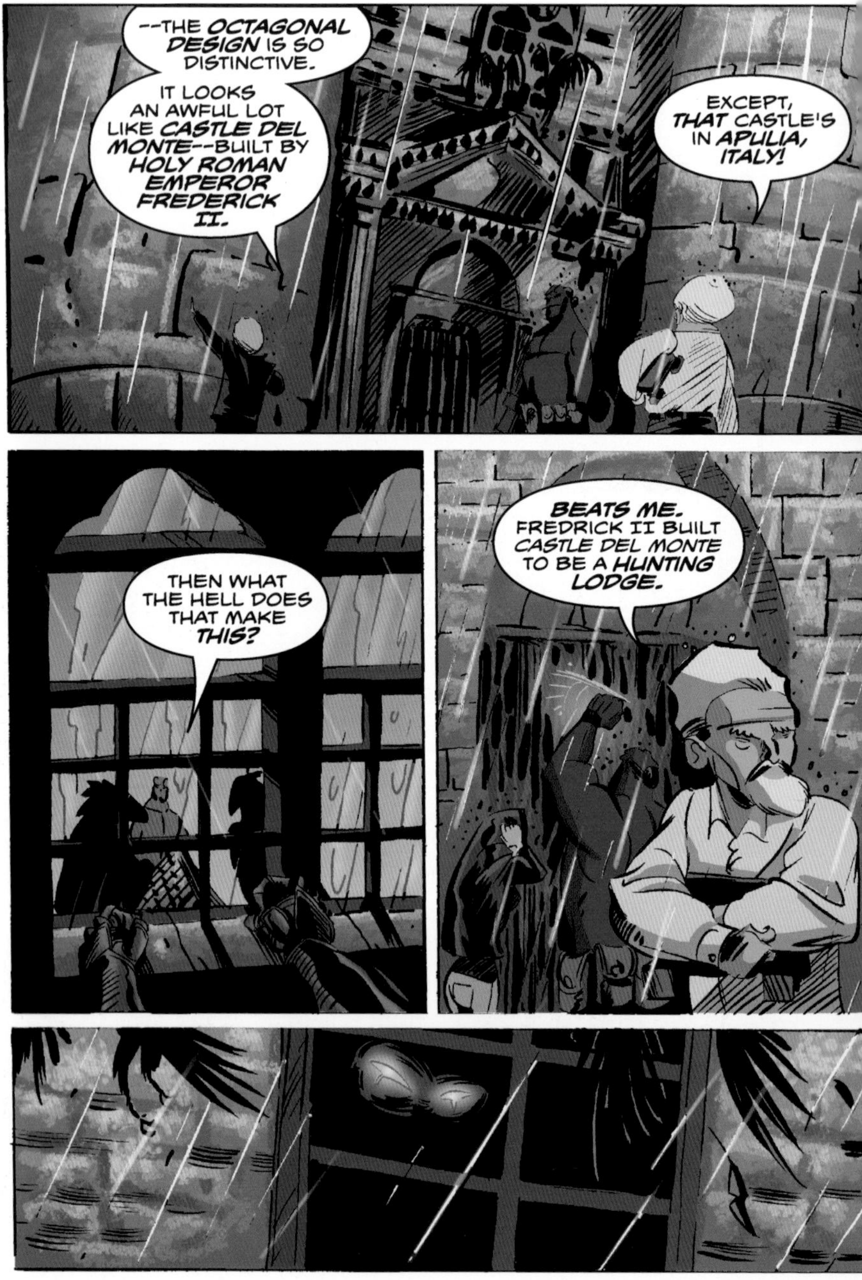
--THE OCTAGONAL DESIGN IS SO DISTINCTIVE.
IT LOOKS AN AWFUL LOT LIKE CASTLE DEL MONTE--BUILT BY HOLY ROMAN EMPEROR FREDERICK II.
EXCEPT, THAT CASTLE'S IN APULIA, ITALY!
THEN WHAT THE HELL DOES THAT MAKE THIS?
BEATS ME. FREDRICK II BUILT CASTLE DEL MONTE TO BE A HUNTING LODGE.

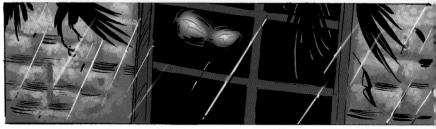

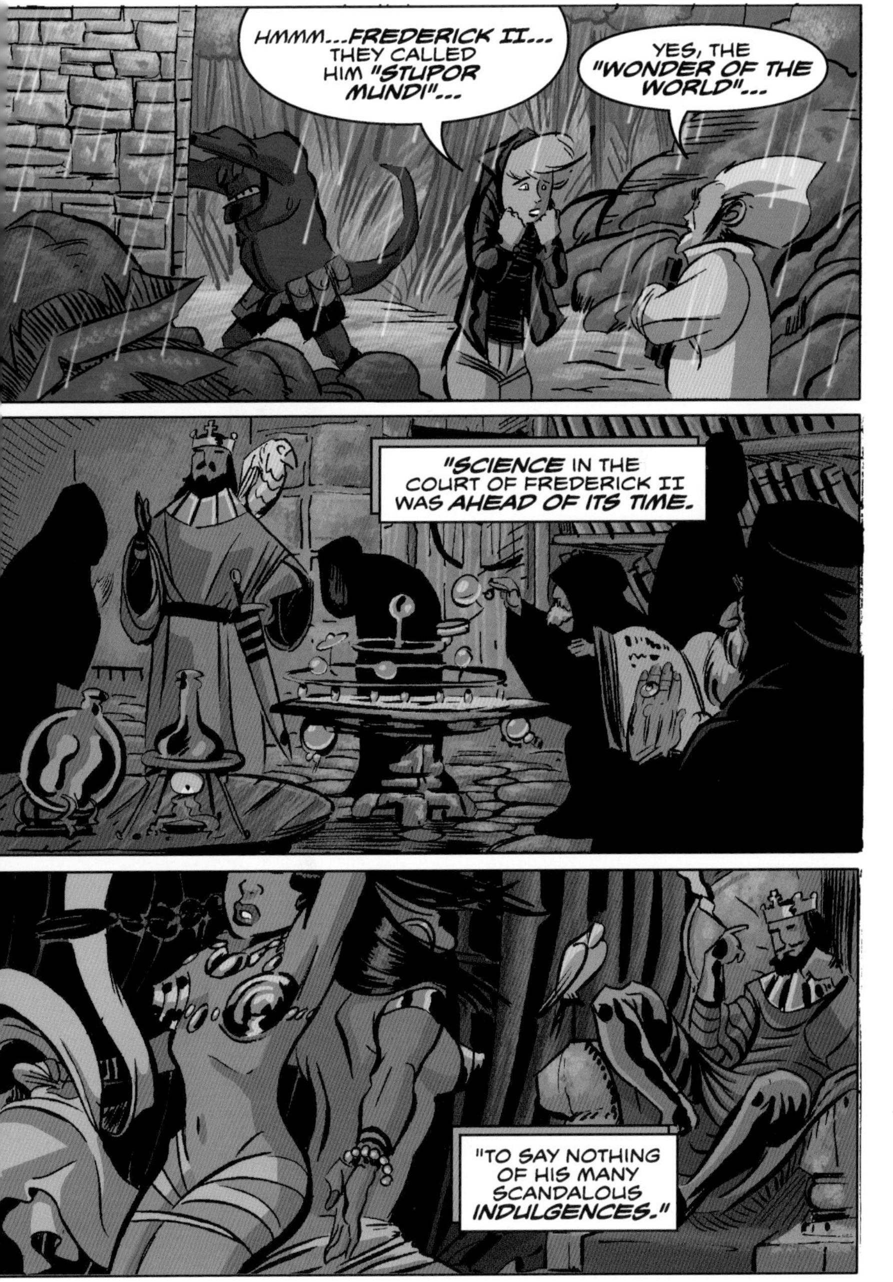
HMMM...FREDERICK II... THEY CALLED HIM "STUPOR MUNDI"...
YES, THE "WONDER OF THE WORLD"...
"SCIENCE IN THE COURT OF FREDERICK II WAS AHEAD OF ITS TIME.
"TO SAY NOTHING OF HIS MANY SCANDALOUS INDULGENCES."

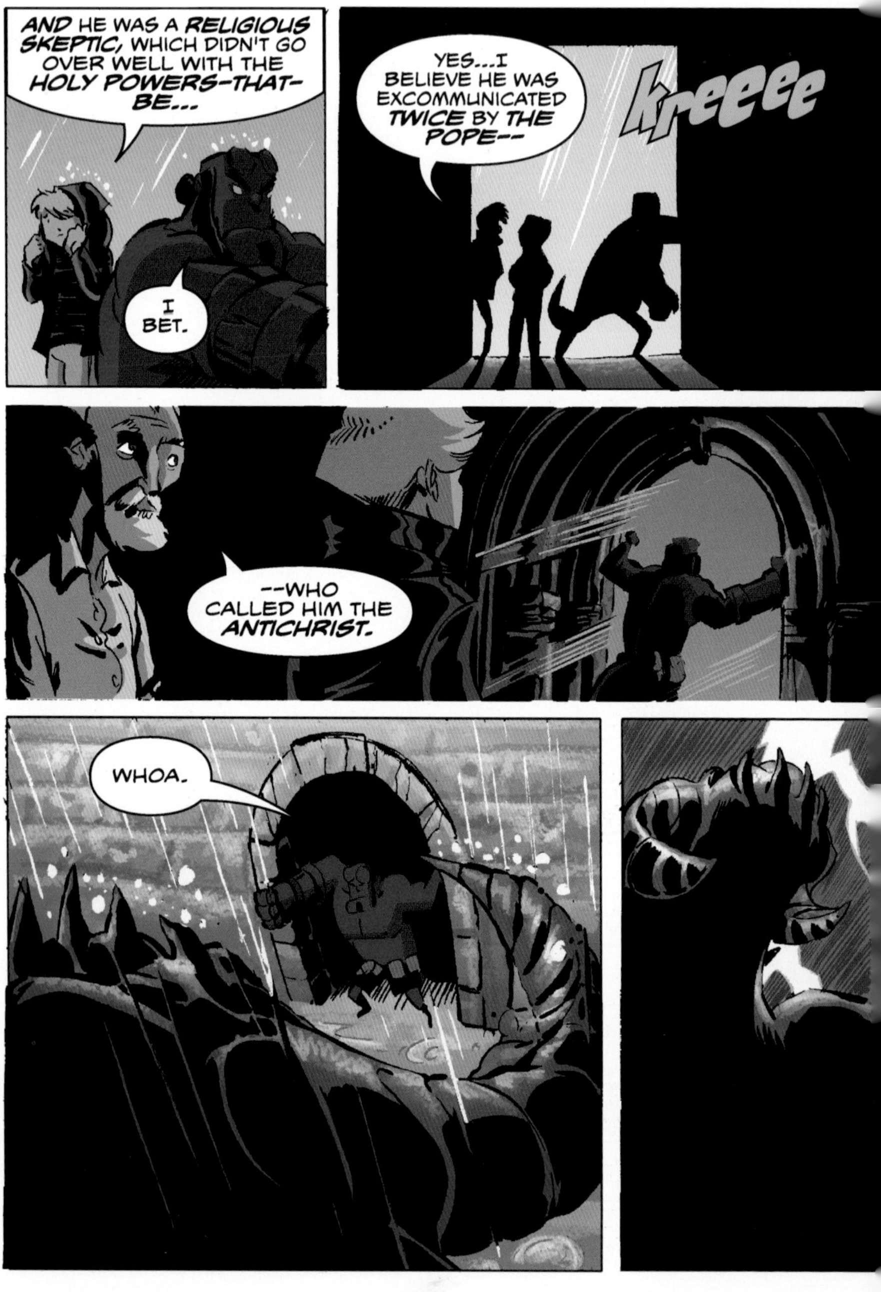
AND HE WAS A RELIGIOUS SKEPTIC, WHICH DIDN'T GO OVER WELL WITH THE HOLY POWERS-THAT-BE...
I BET.
YES...I BELIEVE HE WAS EXCOMMUNICATED TWICE BY THE POPE--
kreeeee
--WHO CALLED HIM THE ANTICHRIST.
WHOA.

OKAY, *THAT'S* NOT NORMAL.

NOTHING EVER IS.

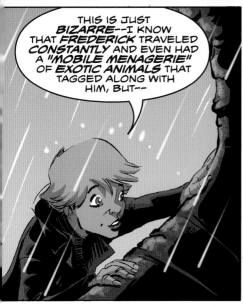

THIS IS JUST *BIZARRE*--I KNOW THAT *FREDERICK* TRAVELED *CONSTANTLY* AND EVEN HAD A *"MOBILE MENAGERIE"* OF *EXOTIC ANIMALS* THAT TAGGED ALONG WITH HIM, BUT--

WELL, MAYBE *THIS* HAS GOT SOMETHING TO DO WITH *THAT.*

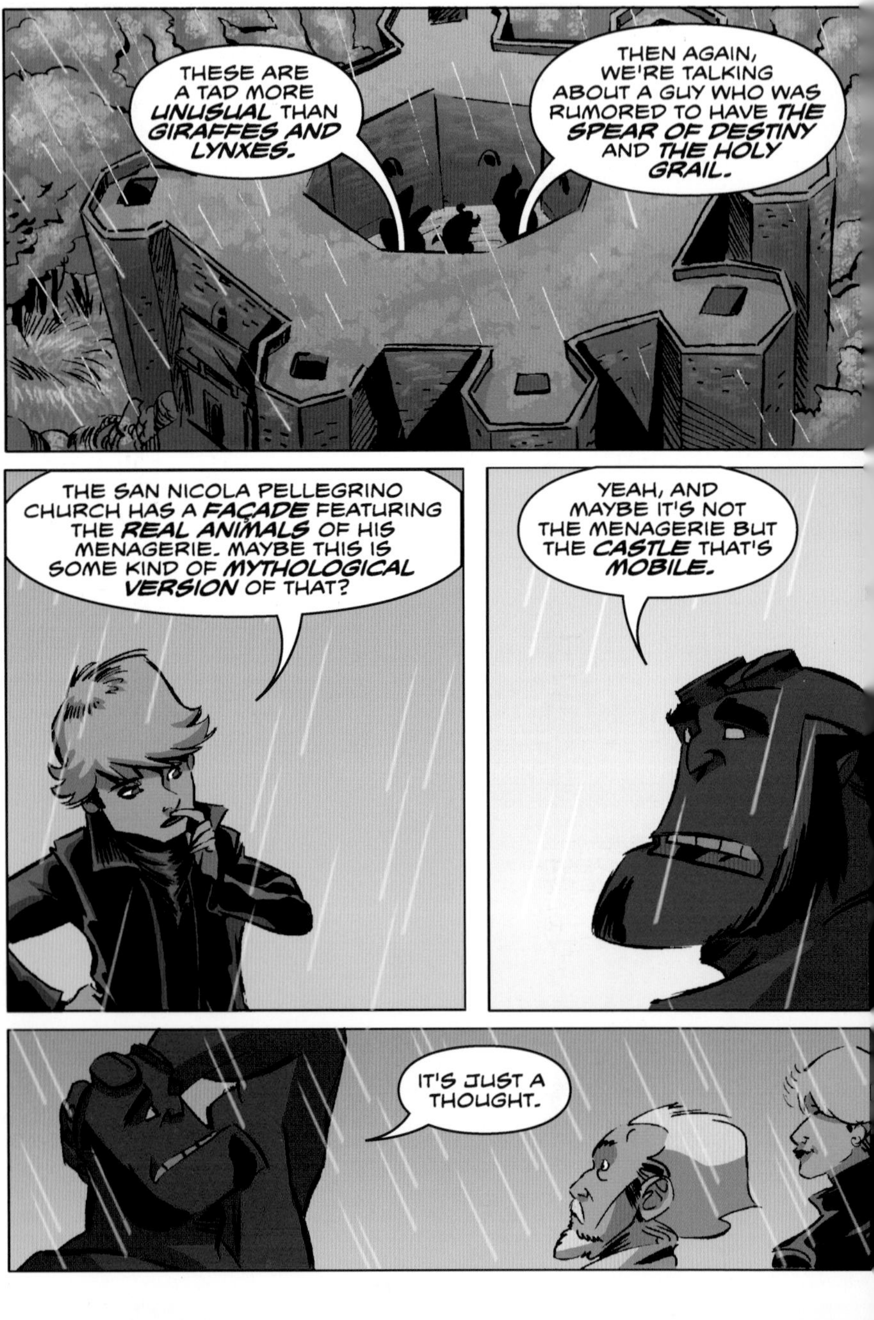
THESE ARE A TAD MORE UNUSUAL THAN GIRAFFES AND LYNXES.
THEN AGAIN, WE'RE TALKING ABOUT A GUY WHO WAS RUMORED TO HAVE THE SPEAR OF DESTINY AND THE HOLY GRAIL.
THE SAN NICOLA PELLEGRINO CHURCH HAS A FAÇADE FEATURING THE REAL ANIMALS OF HIS MENAGERIE. MAYBE THIS IS SOME KIND OF MYTHOLOGICAL VERSION OF THAT?
YEAH, AND MAYBE IT'S NOT THE MENAGERIE BUT THE CASTLE THAT'S MOBILE.
IT'S JUST A THOUGHT.

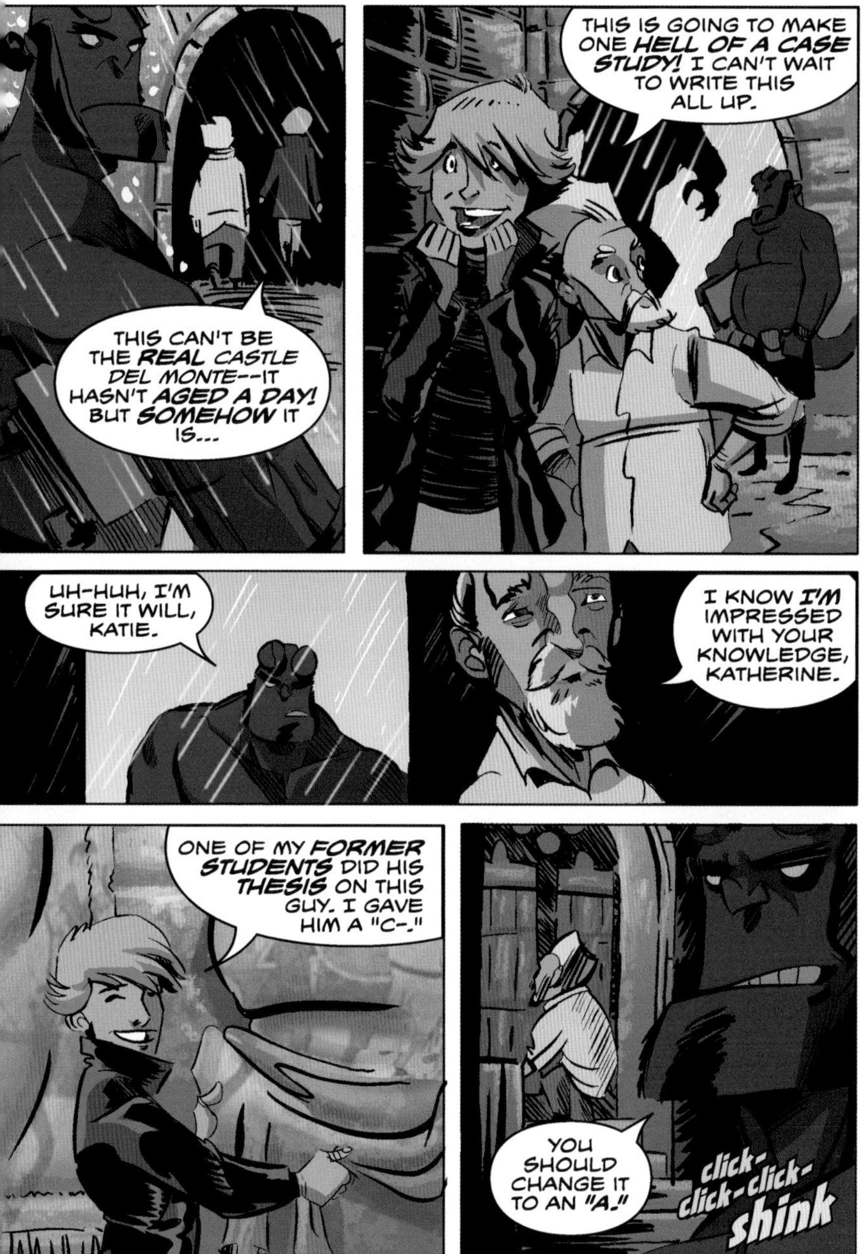
THIS CAN'T BE THE REAL CASTLE DEL MONTE--IT HASN'T AGED A DAY! BUT SOMEHOW IT IS...
THIS IS GOING TO MAKE ONE HELL OF A CASE STUDY! I CAN'T WAIT TO WRITE THIS ALL UP.
UH-HUH, I'M SURE IT WILL, KATIE.
I KNOW I'M IMPRESSED WITH YOUR KNOWLEDGE, KATHERINE.
ONE OF MY FORMER STUDENTS DID HIS THESIS ON THIS GUY. I GAVE HIM A "C-."
YOU SHOULD CHANGE IT TO AN "A."
click-click-click-shink

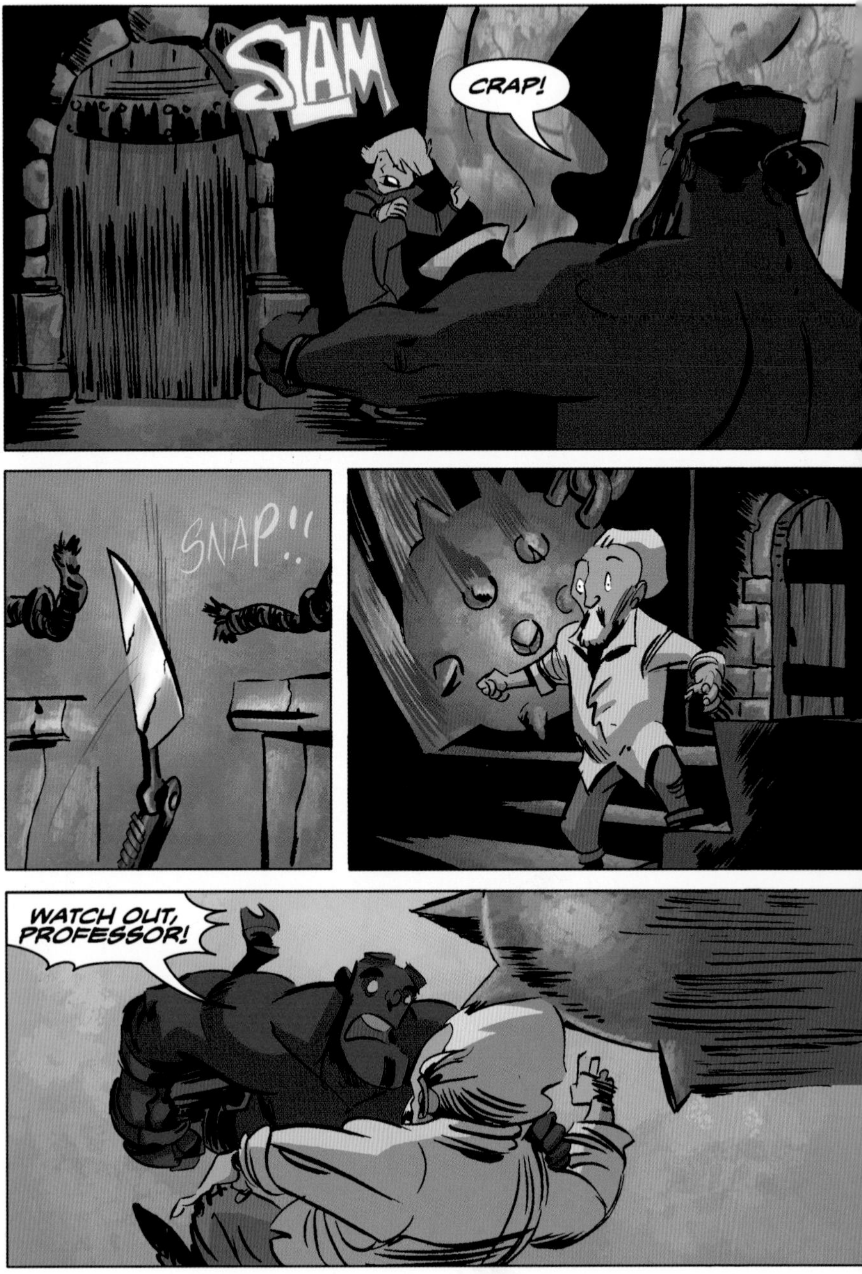
SLAM
CRAP!
SNAP!!
WATCH OUT, PROFESSOR!

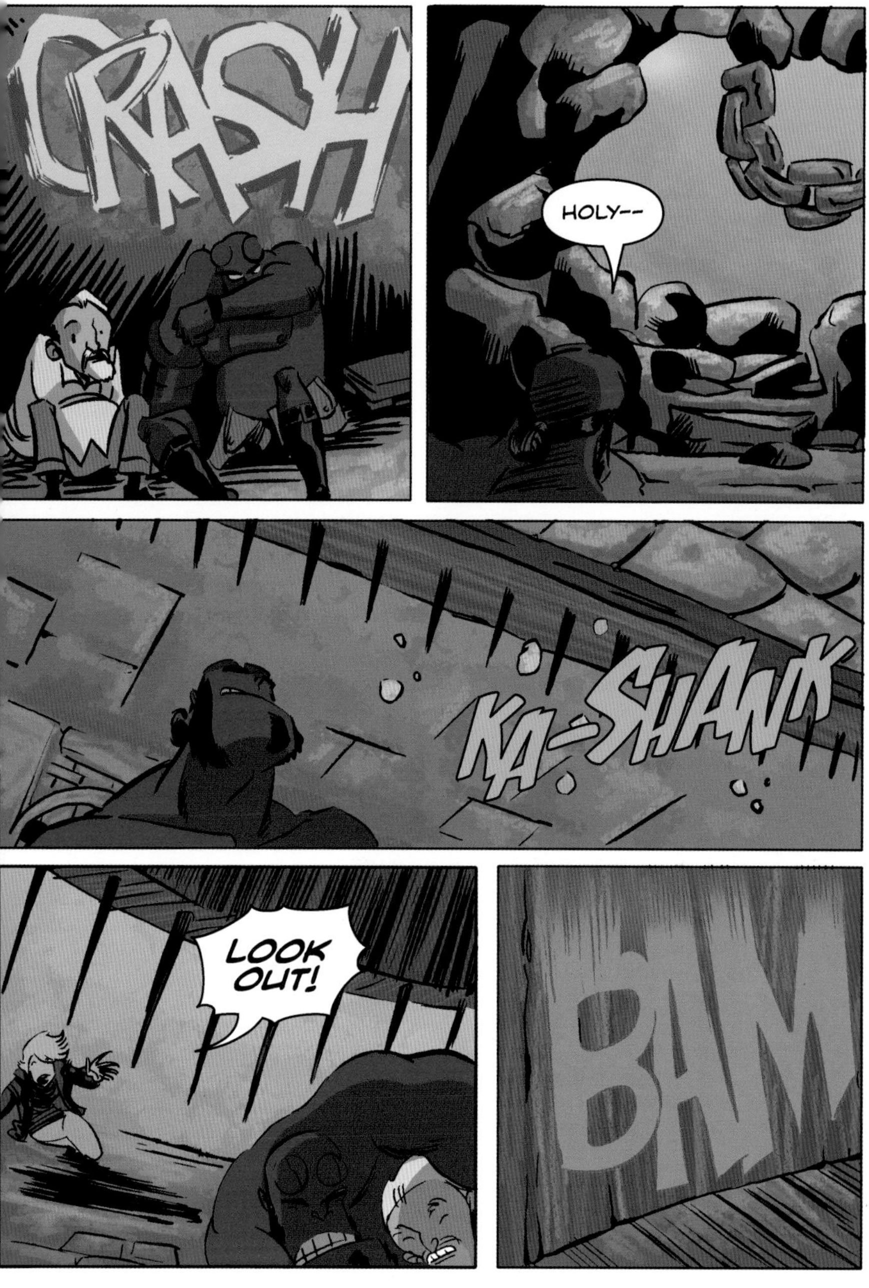
CRASH
HOLY--
KA-SHANK
LOOK OUT!
BAM

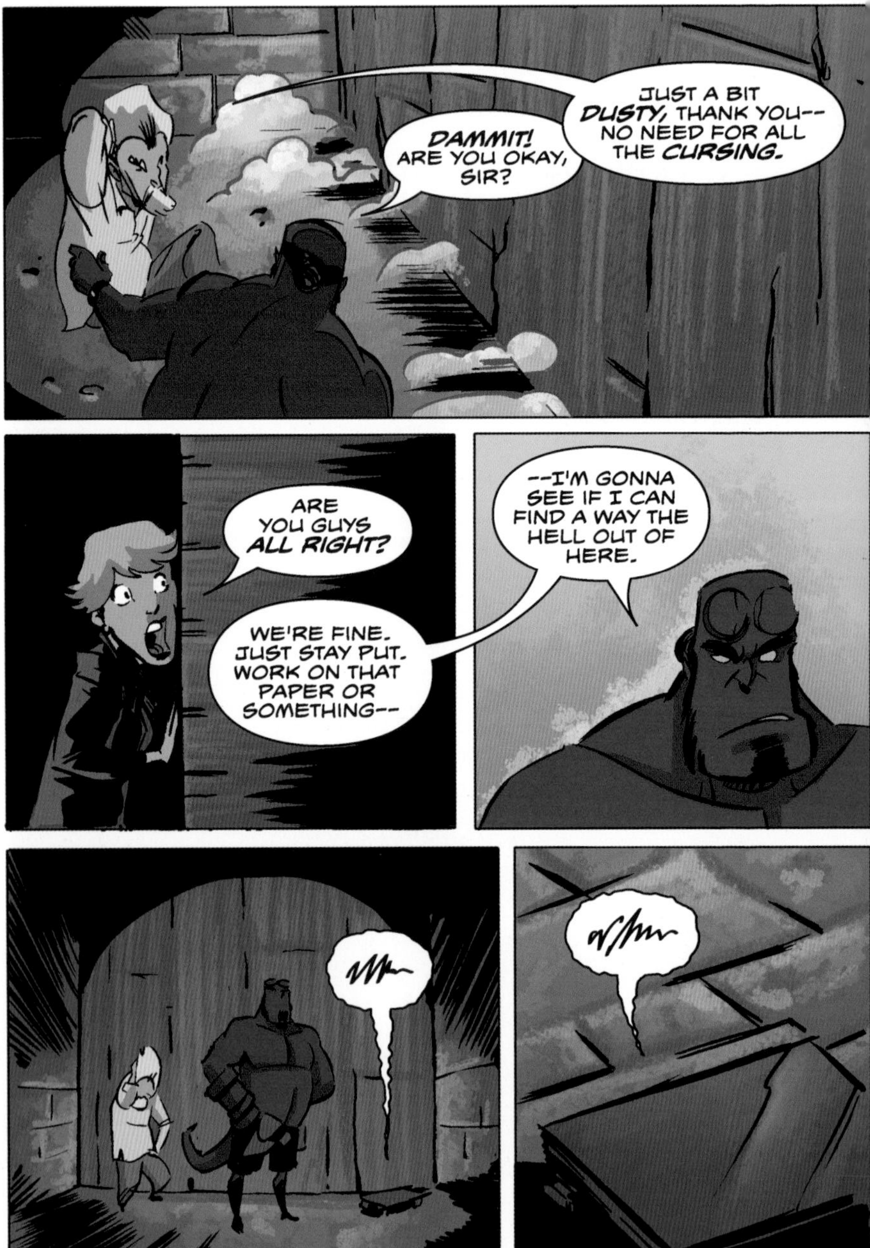
DAMMIT! ARE YOU OKAY, SIR?
JUST A BIT DUSTY, THANK YOU-- NO NEED FOR ALL THE CURSING.
ARE YOU GUYS ALL RIGHT?
WE'RE FINE. JUST STAY PUT. WORK ON THAT PAPER OR SOMETHING--
--I'M GONNA SEE IF I CAN FIND A WAY THE HELL OUT OF HERE.

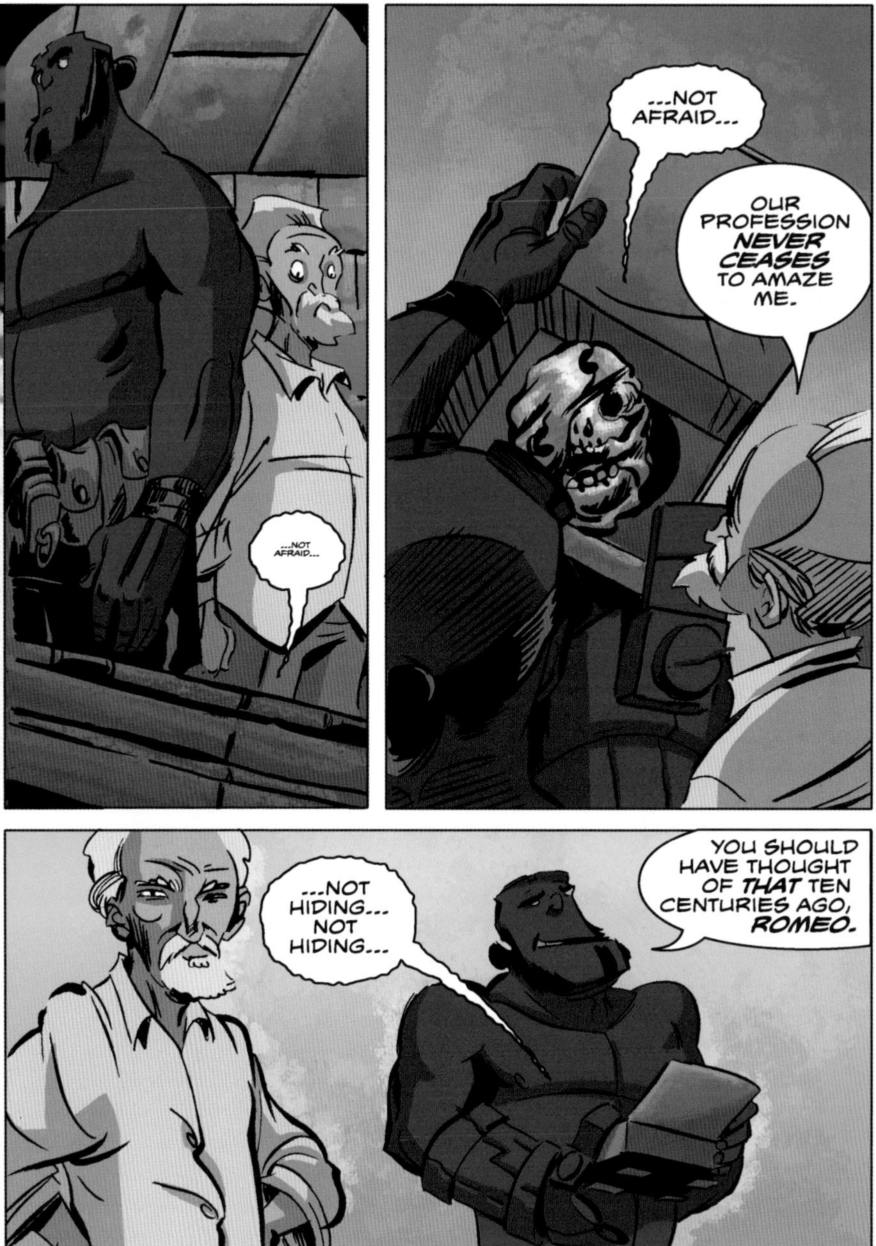
...NOT AFRAID...
...NOT AFRAID...
OUR PROFESSION NEVER CEASES TO AMAZE ME.
...NOT HIDING... NOT HIDING...
YOU SHOULD HAVE THOUGHT OF THAT TEN CENTURIES AGO, ROMEO.

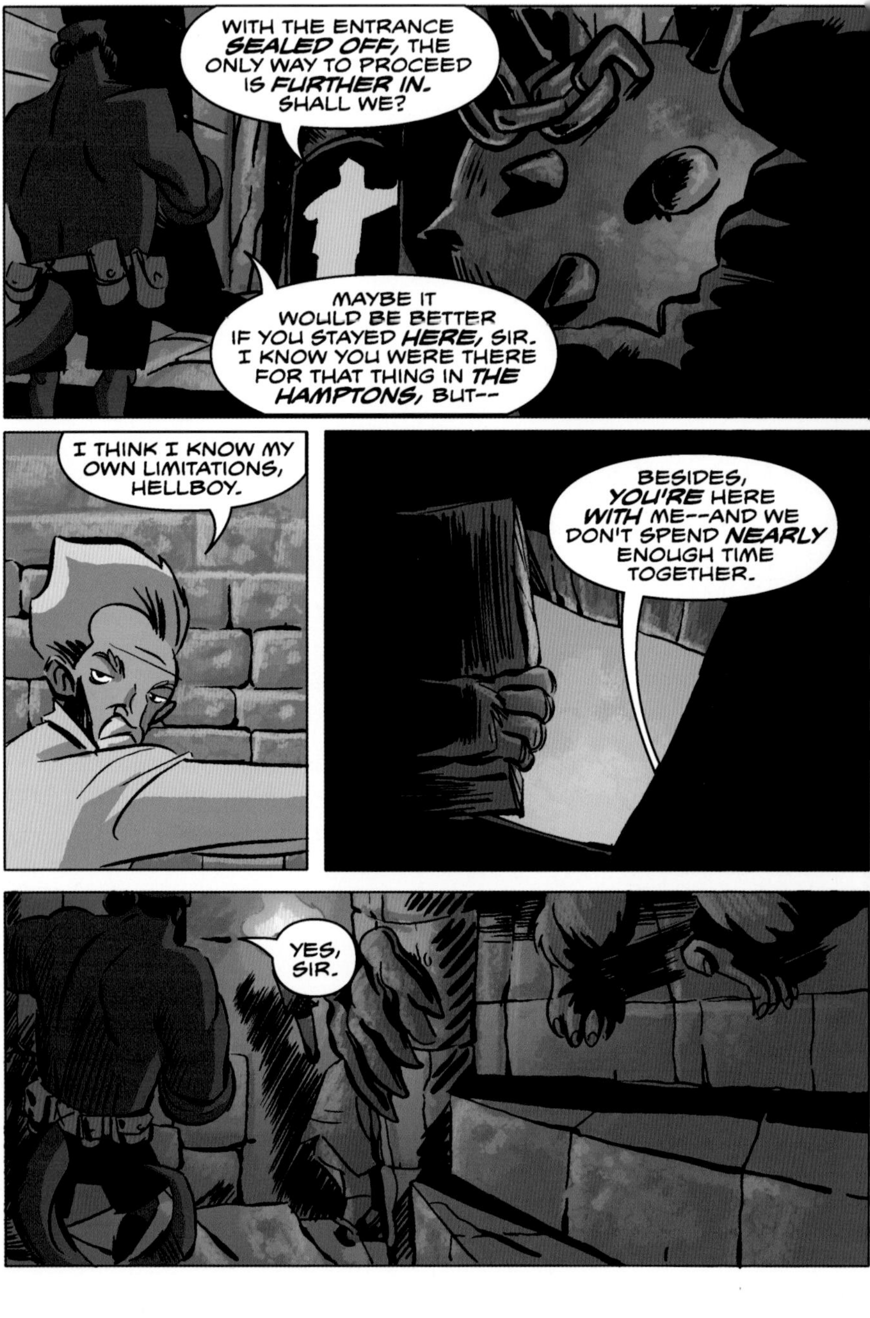
WITH THE ENTRANCE SEALED OFF, THE ONLY WAY TO PROCEED IS FURTHER IN. SHALL WE?
MAYBE IT WOULD BE BETTER IF YOU STAYED HERE, SIR. I KNOW YOU WERE THERE FOR THAT THING IN THE HAMPTONS, BUT--
I THINK I KNOW MY OWN LIMITATIONS, HELLBOY.
BESIDES, YOU'RE HERE WITH ME--AND WE DON'T SPEND NEARLY ENOUGH TIME TOGETHER.
YES, SIR.

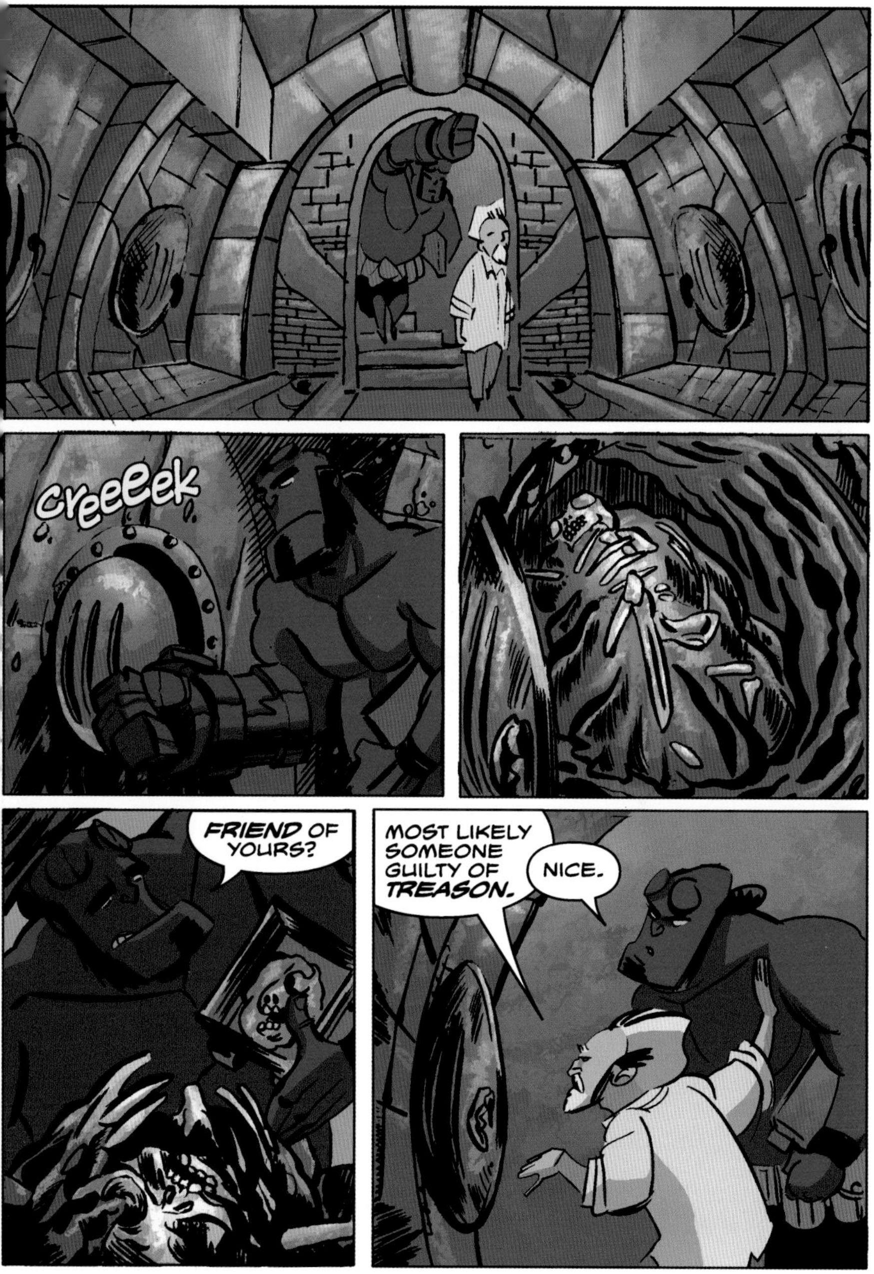
creeeek
FRIEND OF YOURS?
MOST LIKELY SOMEONE GUILTY OF TREASON.
NICE.

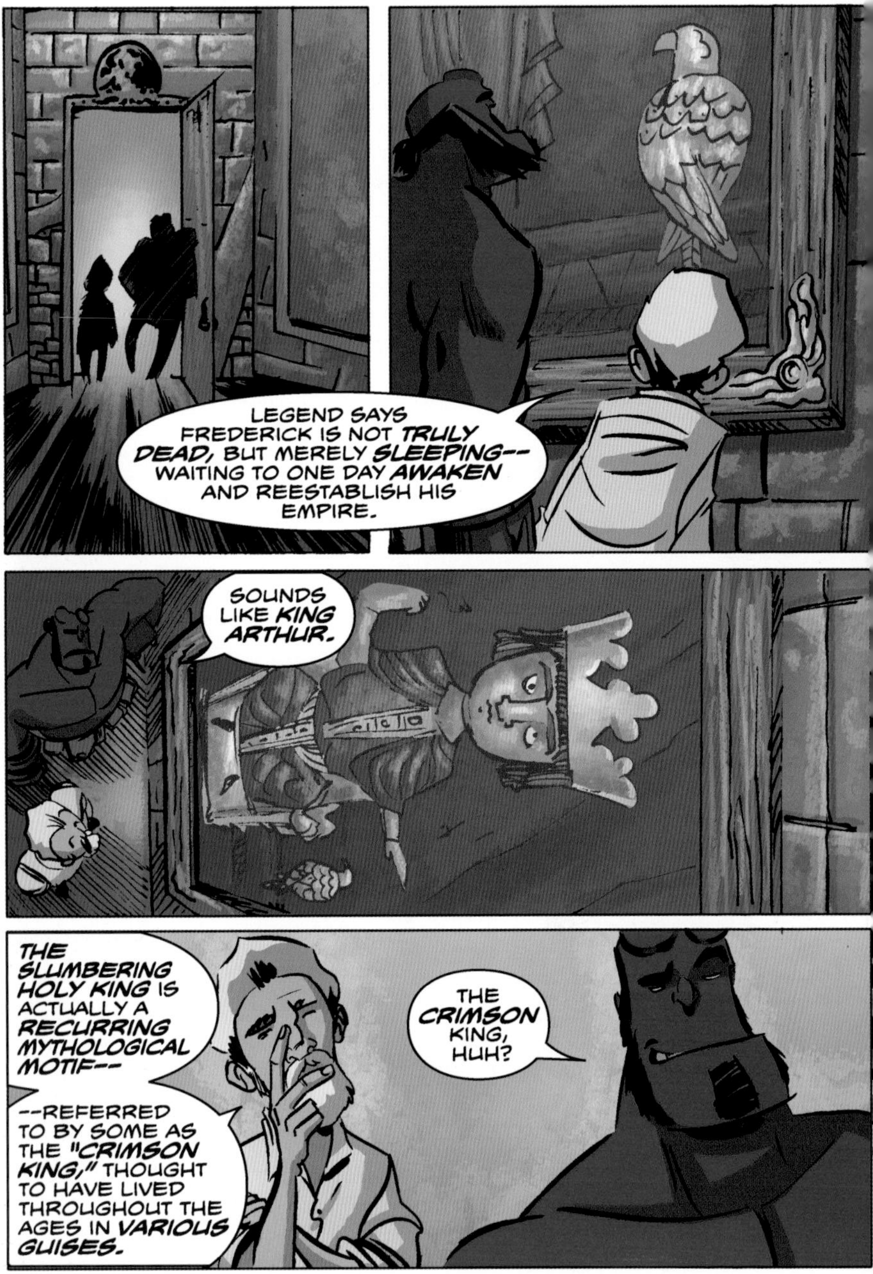
LEGEND SAYS FREDERICK IS NOT TRULY DEAD, BUT MERELY SLEEPING-- WAITING TO ONE DAY AWAKEN AND REESTABLISH HIS EMPIRE.
SOUNDS LIKE KING ARTHUR.
THE SLUMBERING HOLY KING IS ACTUALLY A RECURRING MYTHOLOGICAL MOTIF--
--REFERRED TO BY SOME AS THE "CRIMSON KING," THOUGHT TO HAVE LIVED THROUGHOUT THE AGES IN VARIOUS GUISES.
THE CRIMSON KING, HUH?

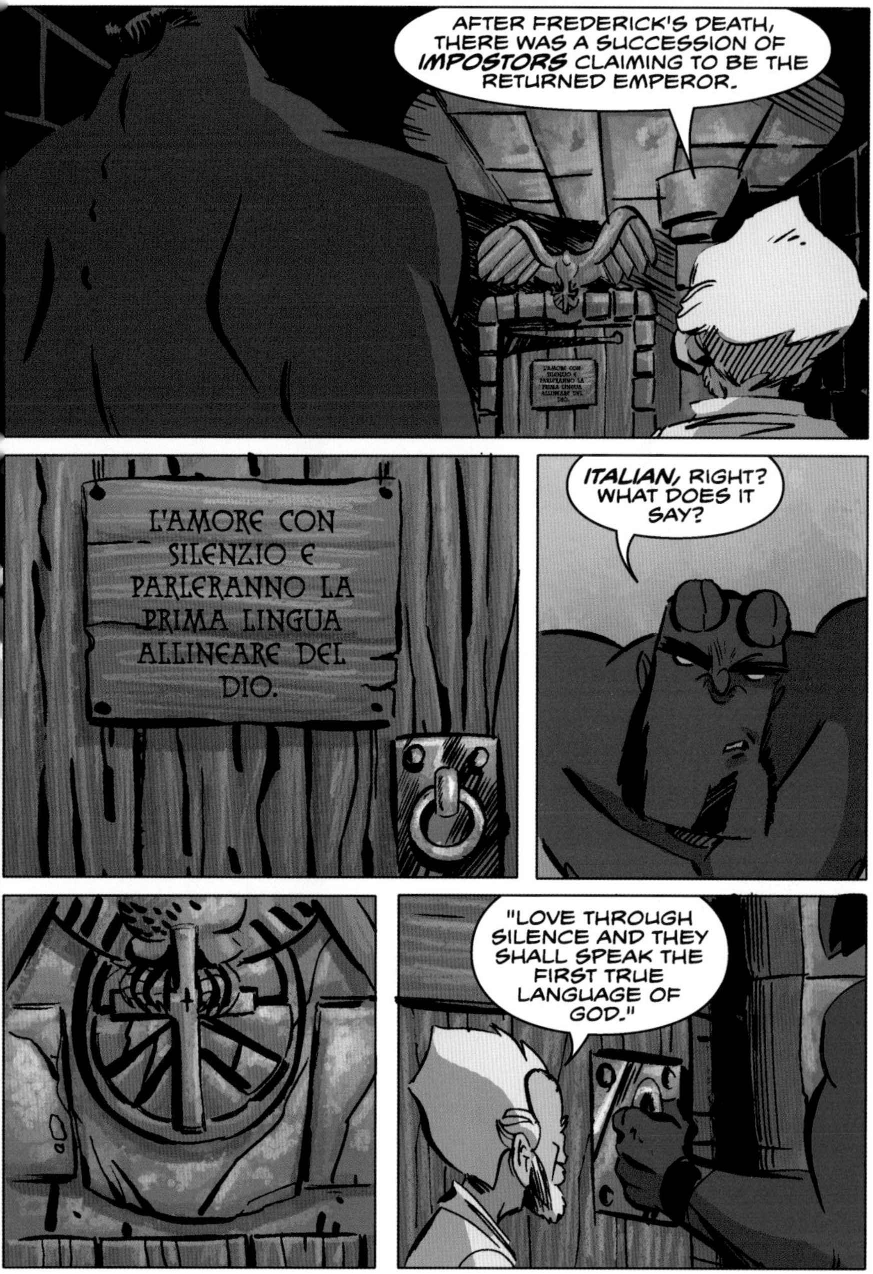
AFTER FREDERICK'S DEATH, THERE WAS A SUCCESSION OF IMPOSTORS CLAIMING TO BE THE RETURNED EMPEROR.
L'AMORE CON SILENZIO E PARLERANNO LA PRIMA LINGUA ALLINEARE DEL DIO.
ITALIAN, RIGHT? WHAT DOES IT SAY?
"LOVE THROUGH SILENCE AND THEY SHALL SPEAK THE FIRST TRUE LANGUAGE OF GOD."

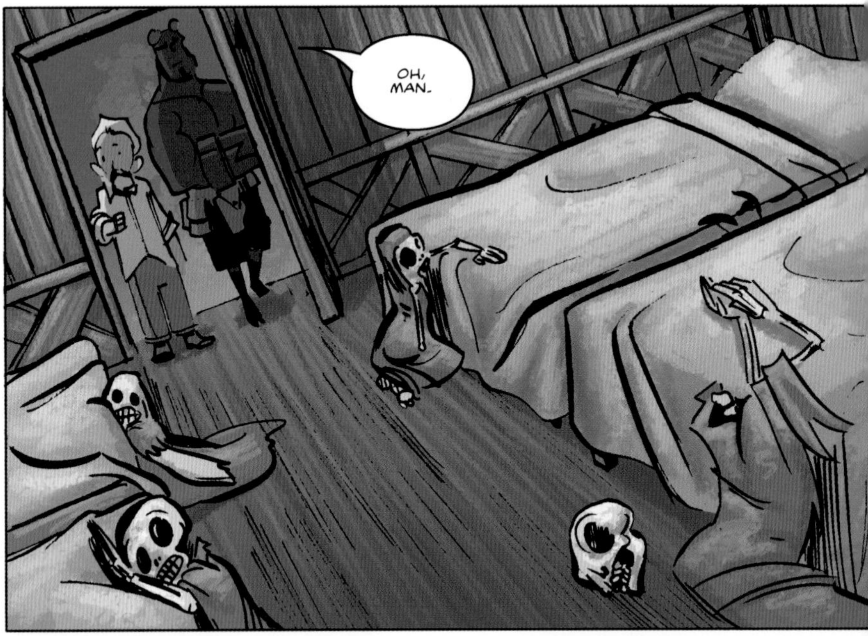
OH, MAN.

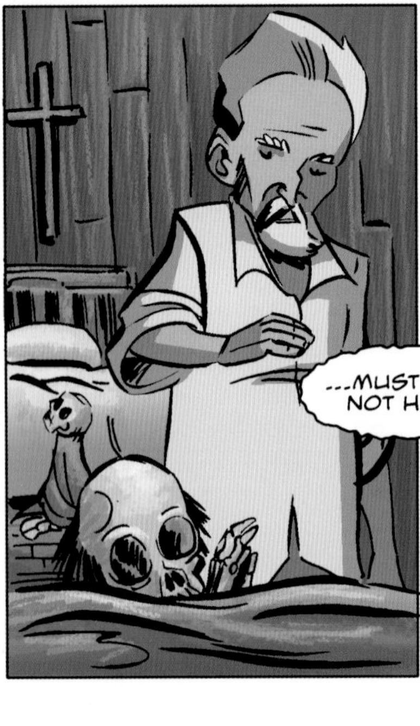
...MUST FIND... NOT HIDE...

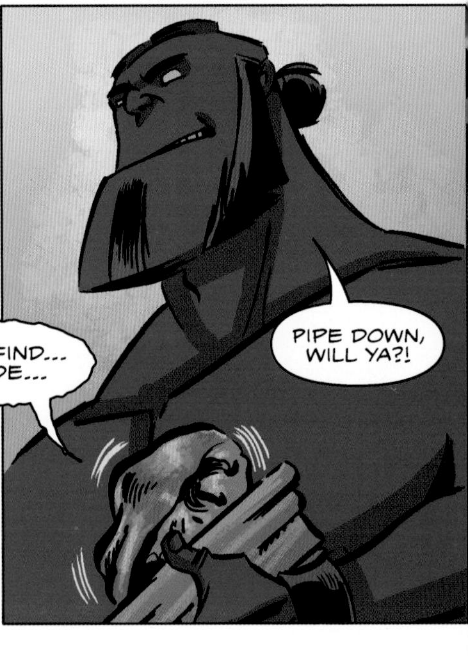
PIPE DOWN, WILL YA?!

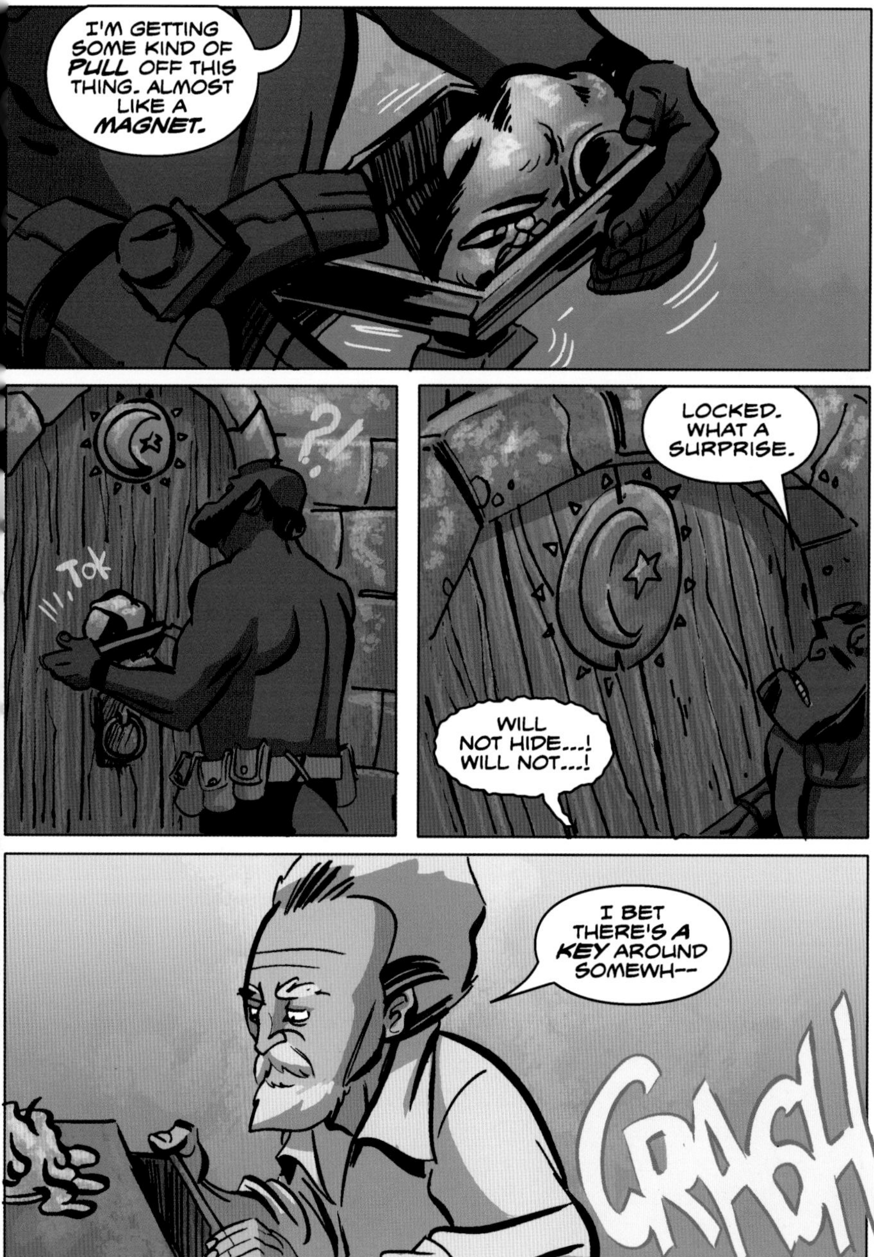
I'M GETTING SOME KIND OF PULL OFF THIS THING. ALMOST LIKE A MAGNET.
?!
TOK
LOCKED. WHAT A SURPRISE.
WILL NOT HIDE...! WILL NOT...!
I BET THERE'S A KEY AROUND SOMEWH--
CRASH

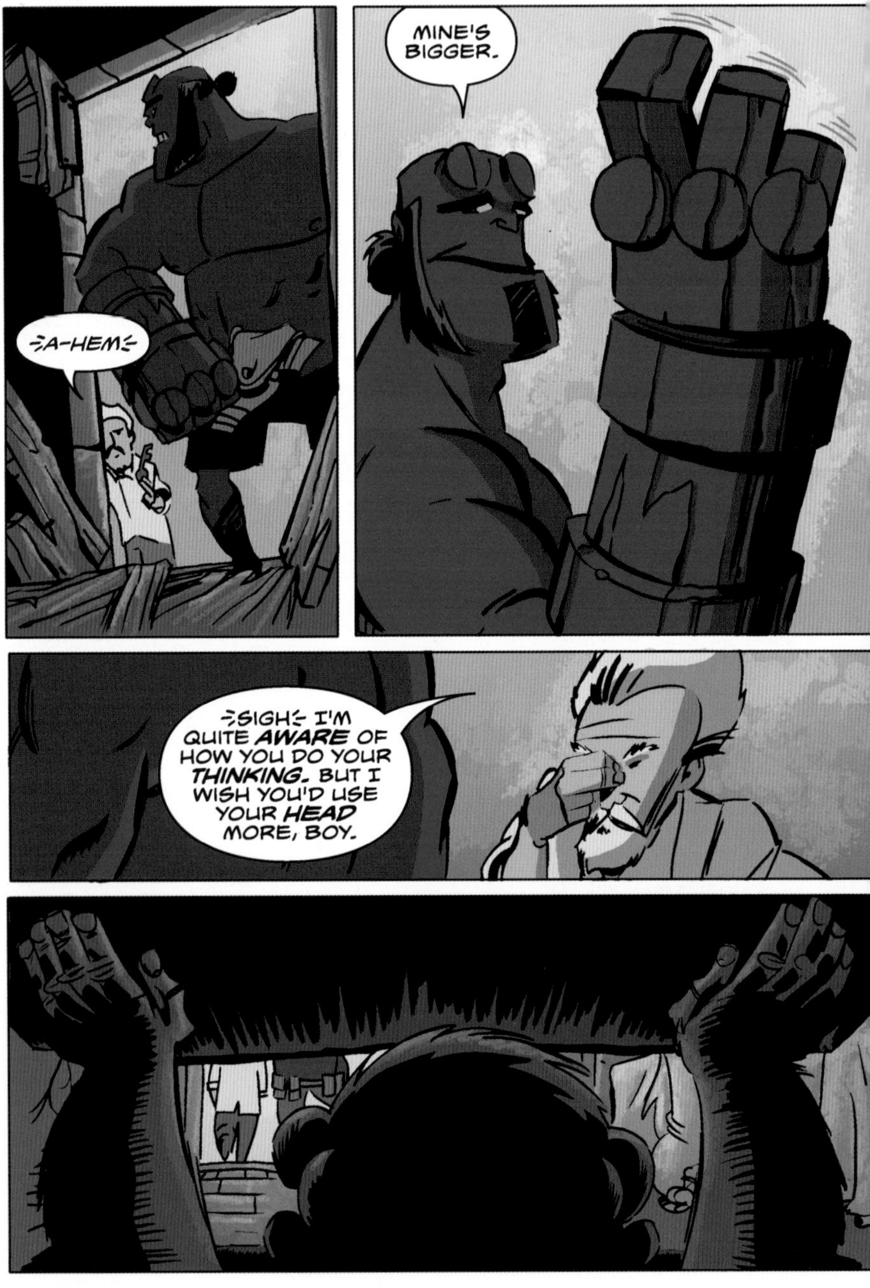
MINE'S BIGGER.
=A-HEM=
=SIGH= I'M QUITE AWARE OF HOW YOU DO YOUR THINKING. BUT I WISH YOU'D USE YOUR HEAD MORE, BOY.

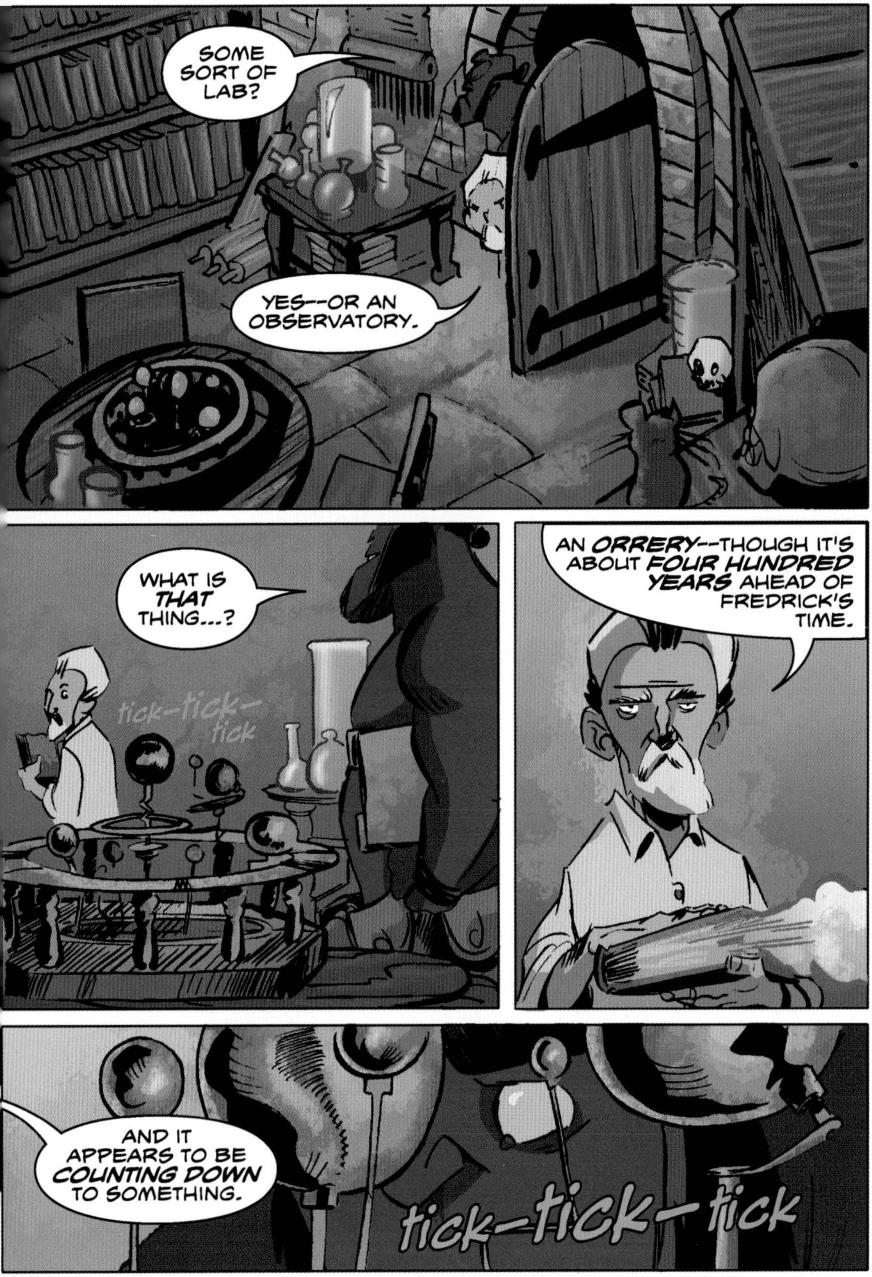
SOME SORT OF LAB?
YES--OR AN OBSERVATORY.
WHAT IS THAT THING...?
tick-tick-tick
AN ORRERY--THOUGH IT'S ABOUT FOUR HUNDRED YEARS AHEAD OF FREDRICK'S TIME.
AND IT APPEARS TO BE COUNTING DOWN TO SOMETHING.
tick-tick-tick

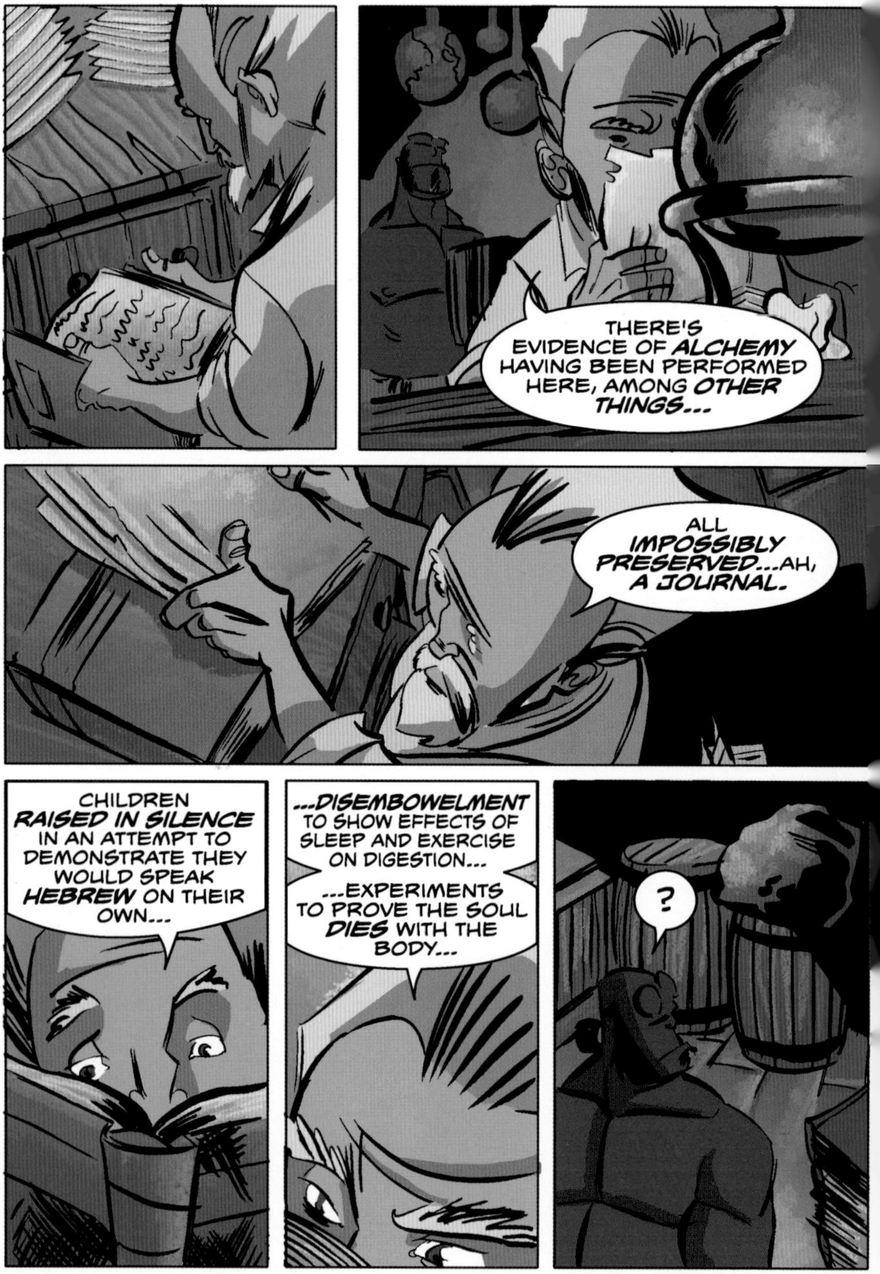
THERE'S EVIDENCE OF ALCHEMY HAVING BEEN PERFORMED HERE, AMONG OTHER THINGS...
ALL IMPOSSIBLY PRESERVED...AH, A JOURNAL.
CHILDREN RAISED IN SILENCE IN AN ATTEMPT TO DEMONSTRATE THEY WOULD SPEAK HEBREW ON THEIR OWN...
...DISEMBOWELMENT TO SHOW EFFECTS OF SLEEP AND EXERCISE ON DIGESTION...
...EXPERIMENTS TO PROVE THE SOUL DIES WITH THE BODY...
?

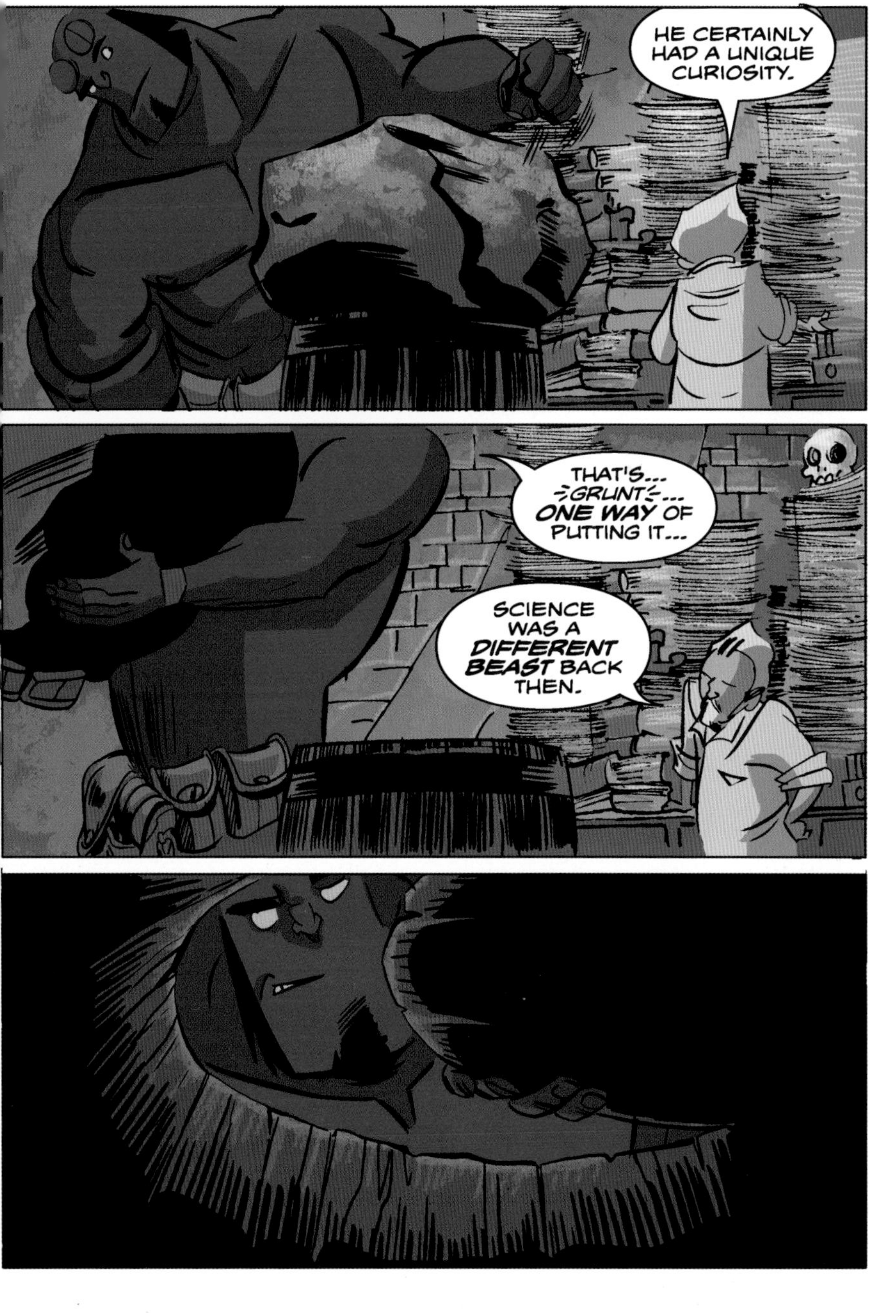
HE CERTAINLY HAD A UNIQUE CURIOSITY.
THAT'S... GRUNT... ONE WAY OF PUTTING IT...
SCIENCE WAS A DIFFERENT BEAST BACK THEN.

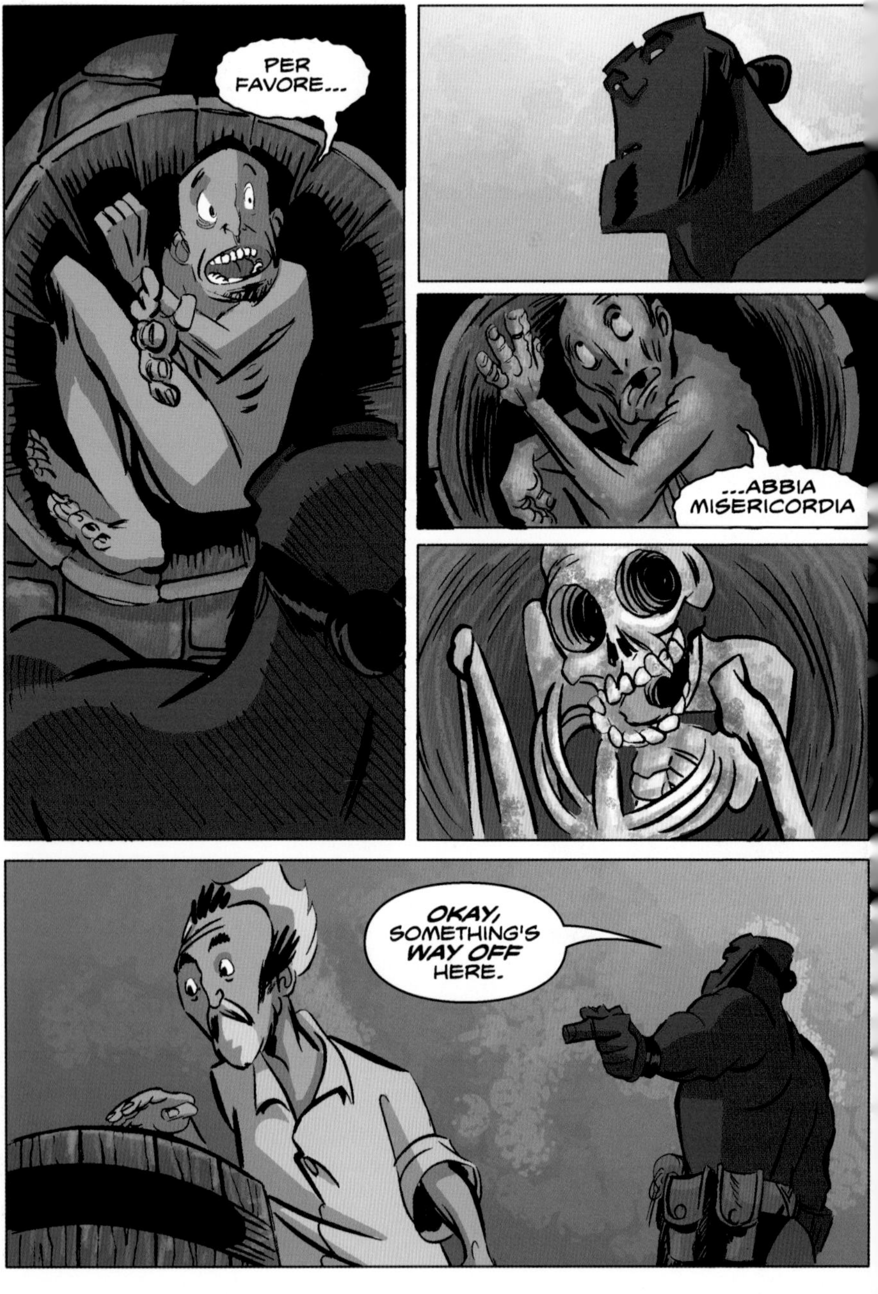
PER FAVORE...
...ABBIA MISERICORDIA
OKAY, SOMETHING'S WAY OFF HERE.

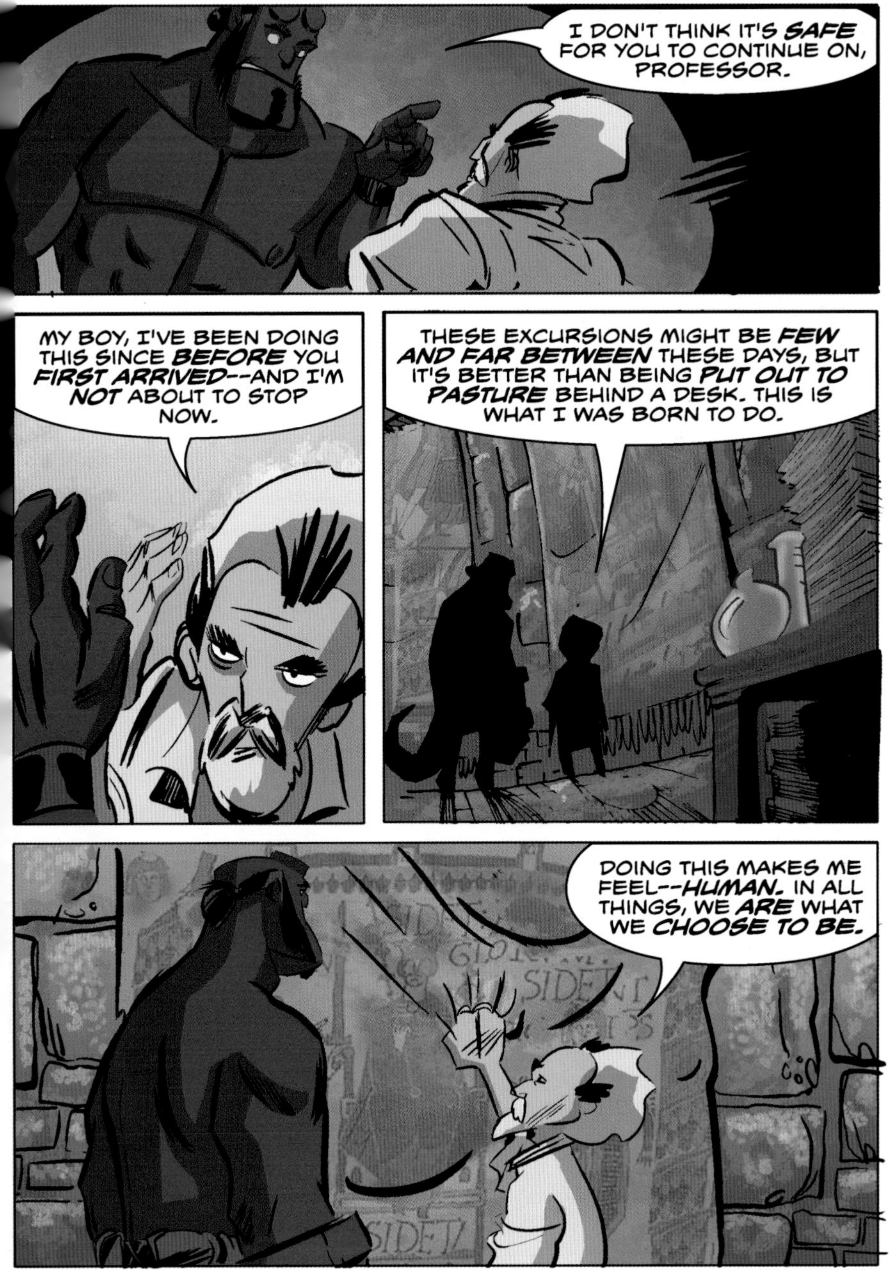
I DON'T THINK IT'S SAFE FOR YOU TO CONTINUE ON, PROFESSOR.
MY BOY, I'VE BEEN DOING THIS SINCE BEFORE YOU FIRST ARRIVED--AND I'M NOT ABOUT TO STOP NOW.
THESE EXCURSIONS MIGHT BE FEW AND FAR BETWEEN THESE DAYS, BUT IT'S BETTER THAN BEING PUT OUT TO PASTURE BEHIND A DESK. THIS IS WHAT I WAS BORN TO DO.
DOING THIS MAKES ME FEEL--HUMAN. IN ALL THINGS, WE ARE WHAT WE CHOOSE TO BE.

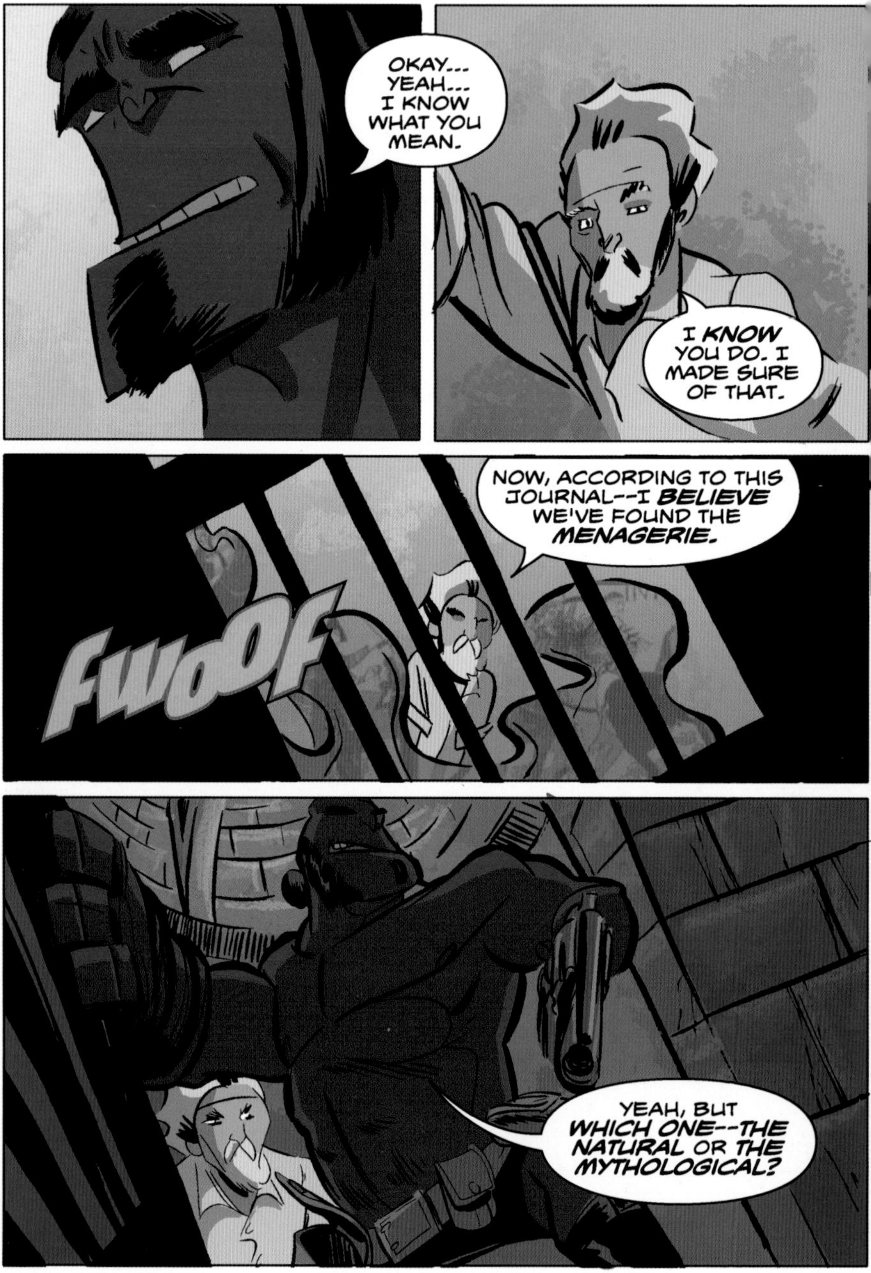
OKAY... YEAH... I KNOW WHAT YOU MEAN.
I KNOW YOU DO. I MADE SURE OF THAT.
NOW, ACCORDING TO THIS JOURNAL--I BELIEVE WE'VE FOUND THE MENAGERIE.
FWOOF
YEAH, BUT WHICH ONE--THE NATURAL OR THE MYTHOLOGICAL?

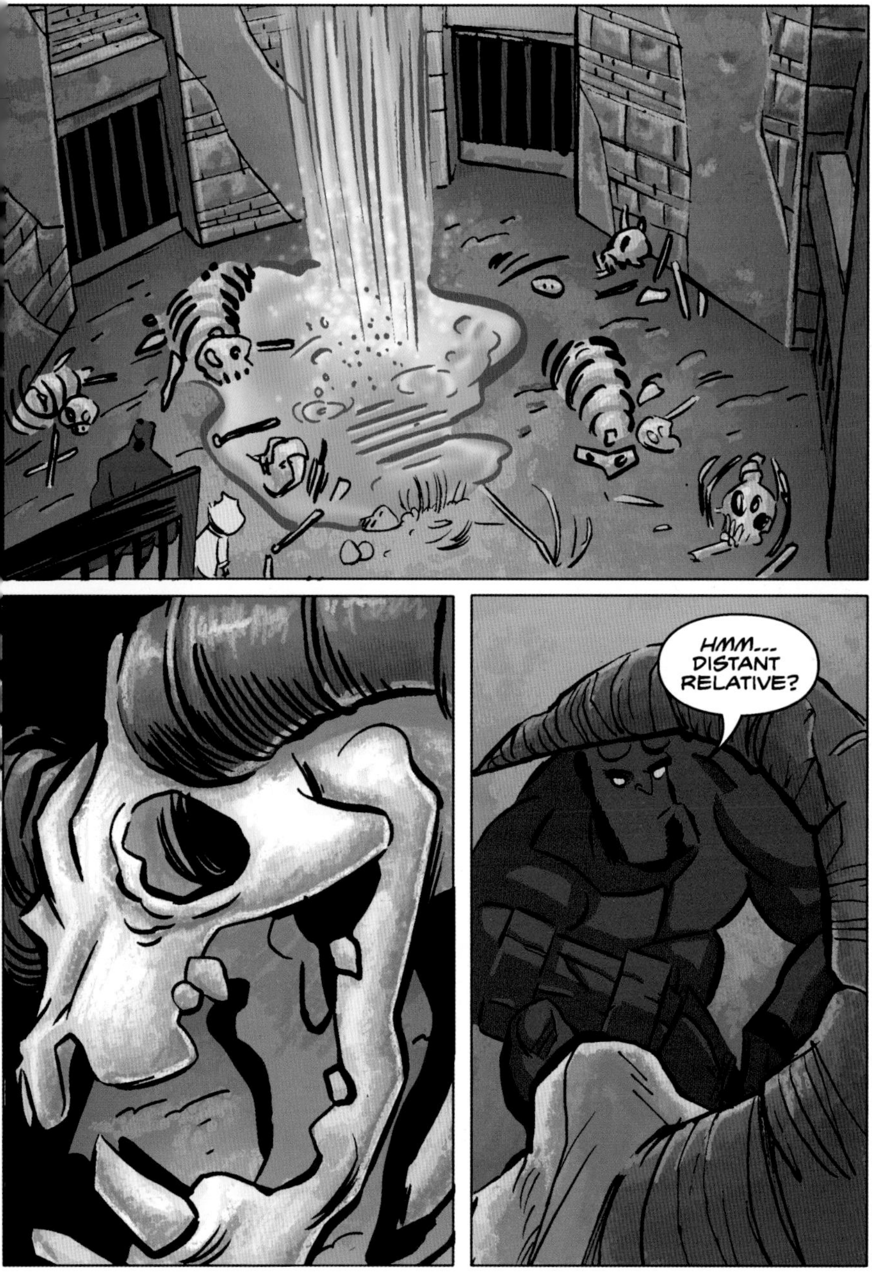
HMM... DISTANT RELATIVE?

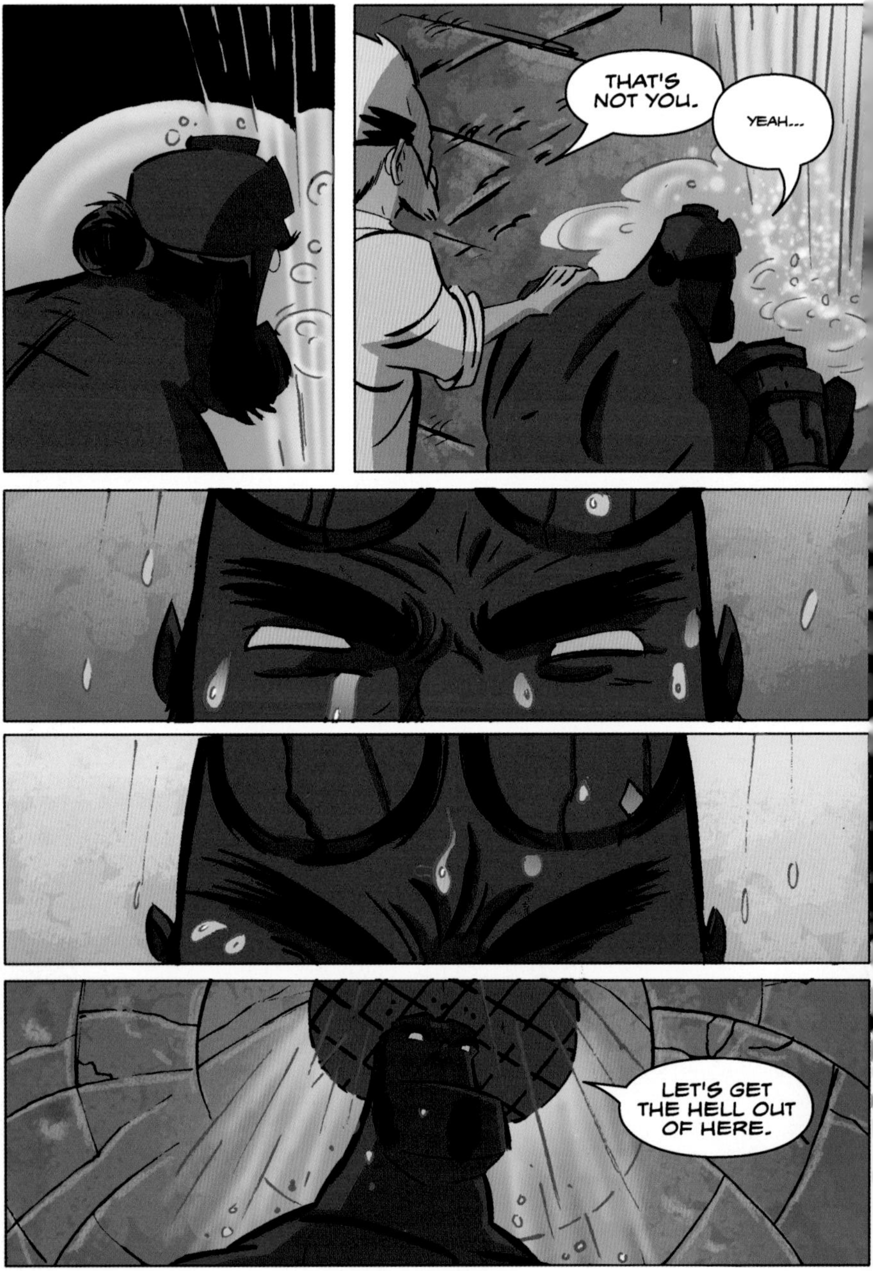
THAT'S NOT YOU.
YEAH...
LET'S GET THE HELL OUT OF HERE.

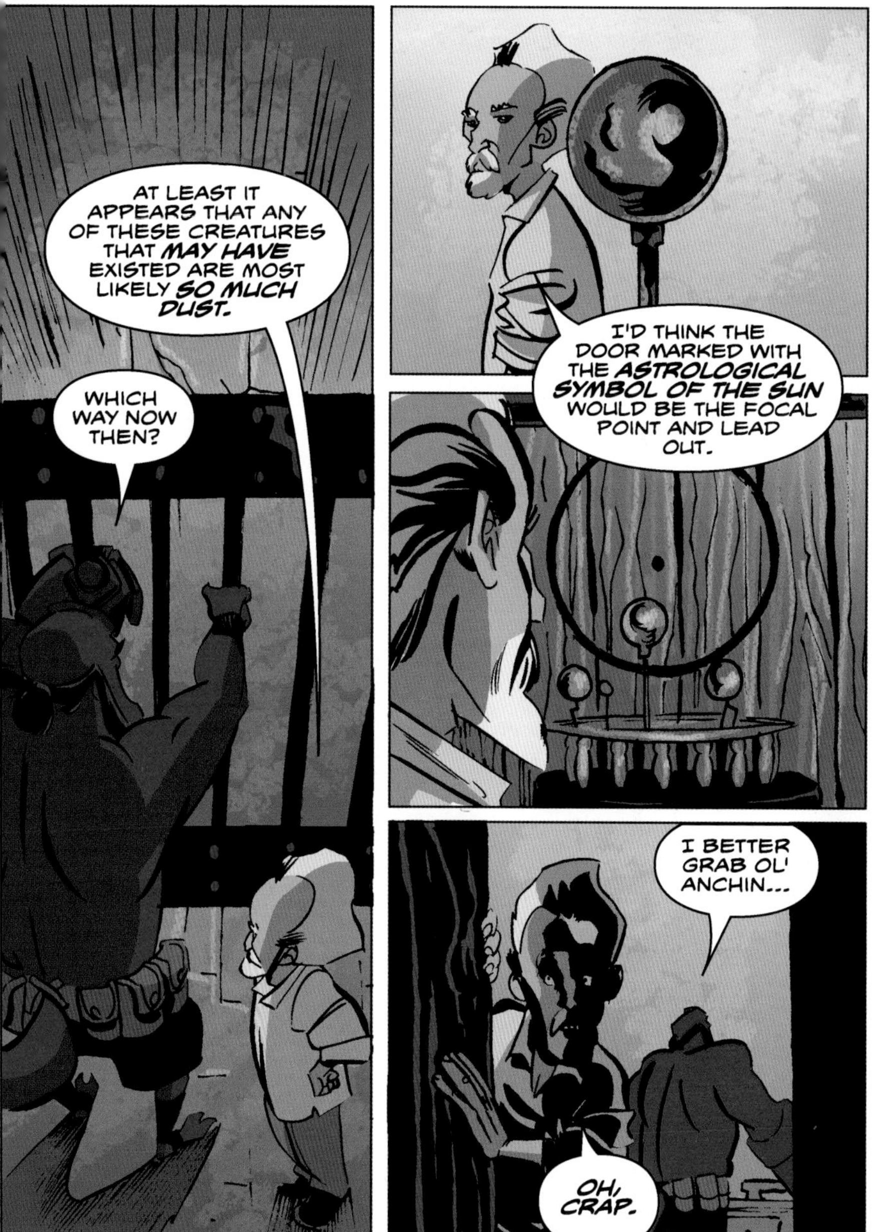
AT LEAST IT APPEARS THAT ANY OF THESE CREATURES THAT MAY HAVE EXISTED ARE MOST LIKELY SO MUCH DUST.
WHICH WAY NOW THEN?
I'D THINK THE DOOR MARKED WITH THE ASTROLOGICAL SYMBOL OF THE SUN WOULD BE THE FOCAL POINT AND LEAD OUT.
I BETTER GRAB OL' ANCHIN...
OH, CRAP.

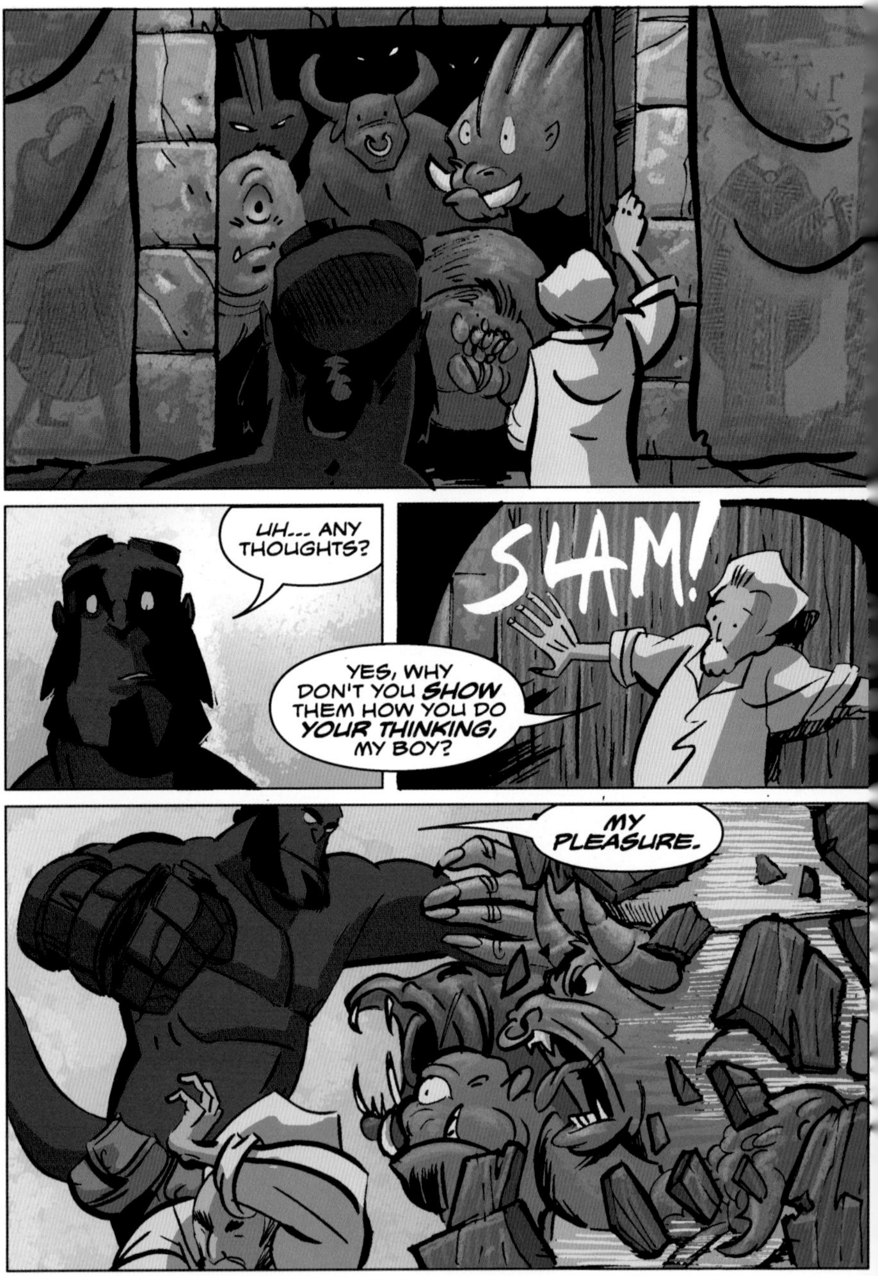
UH... ANY THOUGHTS?
SLAM!
YES, WHY DON'T YOU SHOW THEM HOW YOU DO YOUR THINKING, MY BOY?
MY PLEASURE.

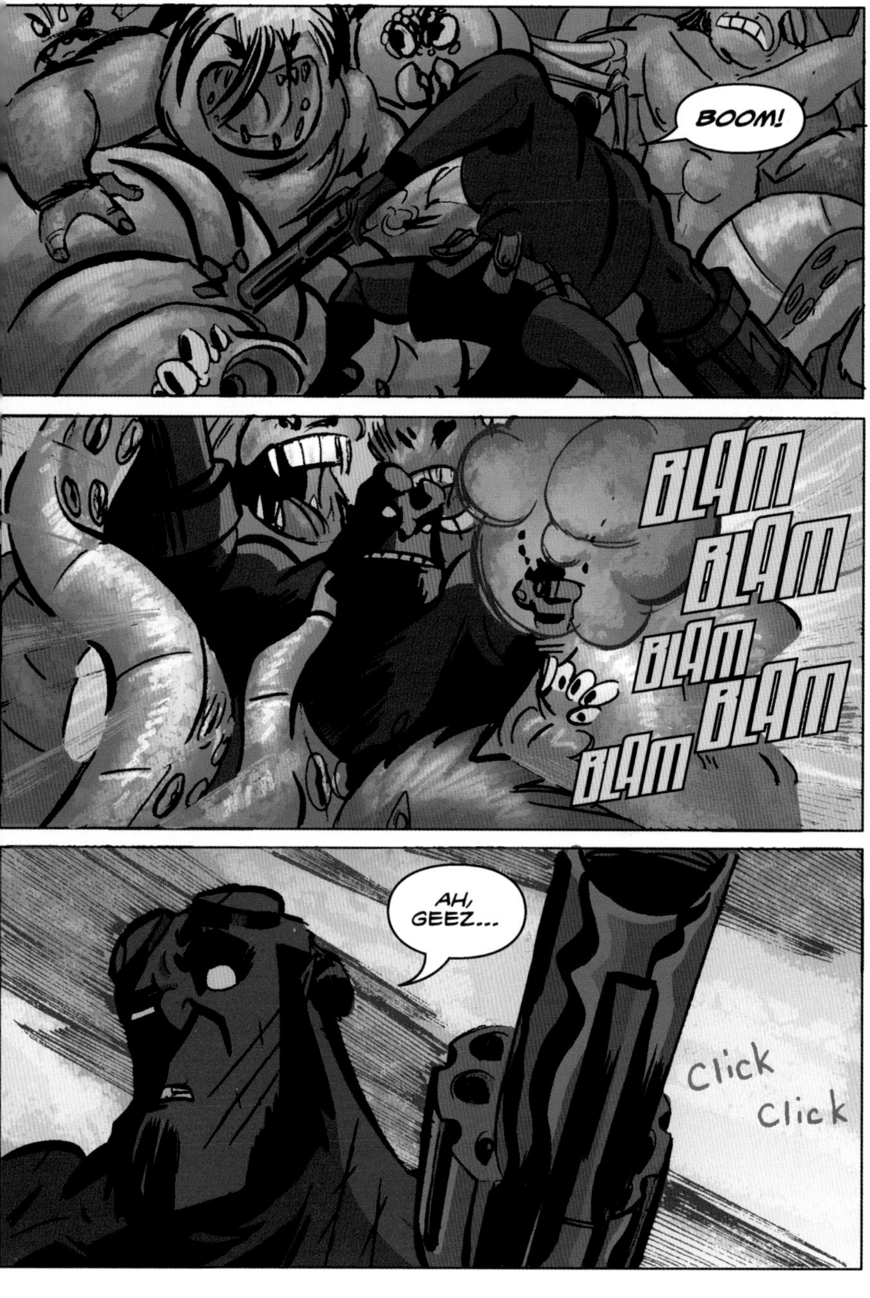
BOOM!
BLAM
BLAM
BLAM
BLAM
BLAM
AH, GEEZ...
Click
Click

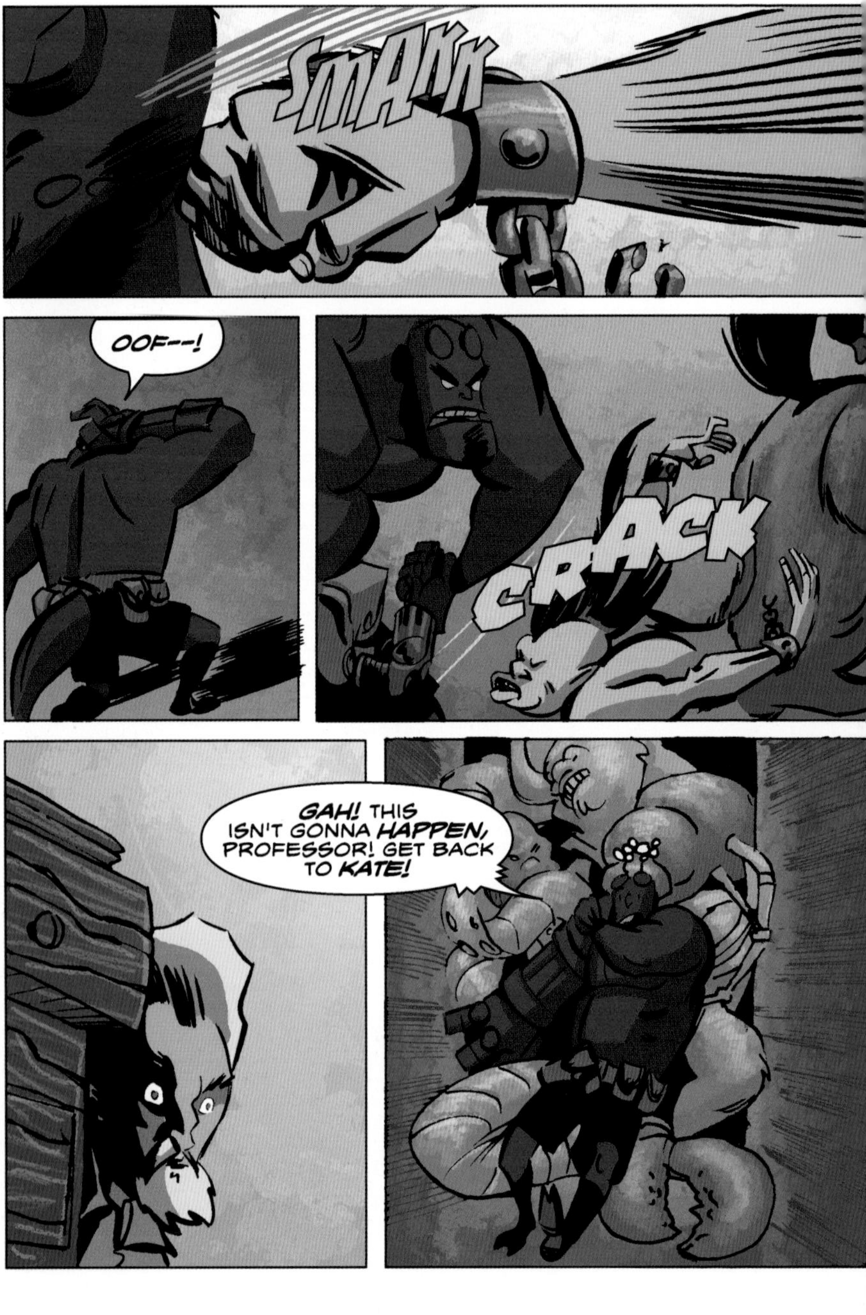
SMAKK
OOF--!
CRACK
GAH! THIS ISN'T GONNA HAPPEN, PROFESSOR! GET BACK TO KATE!

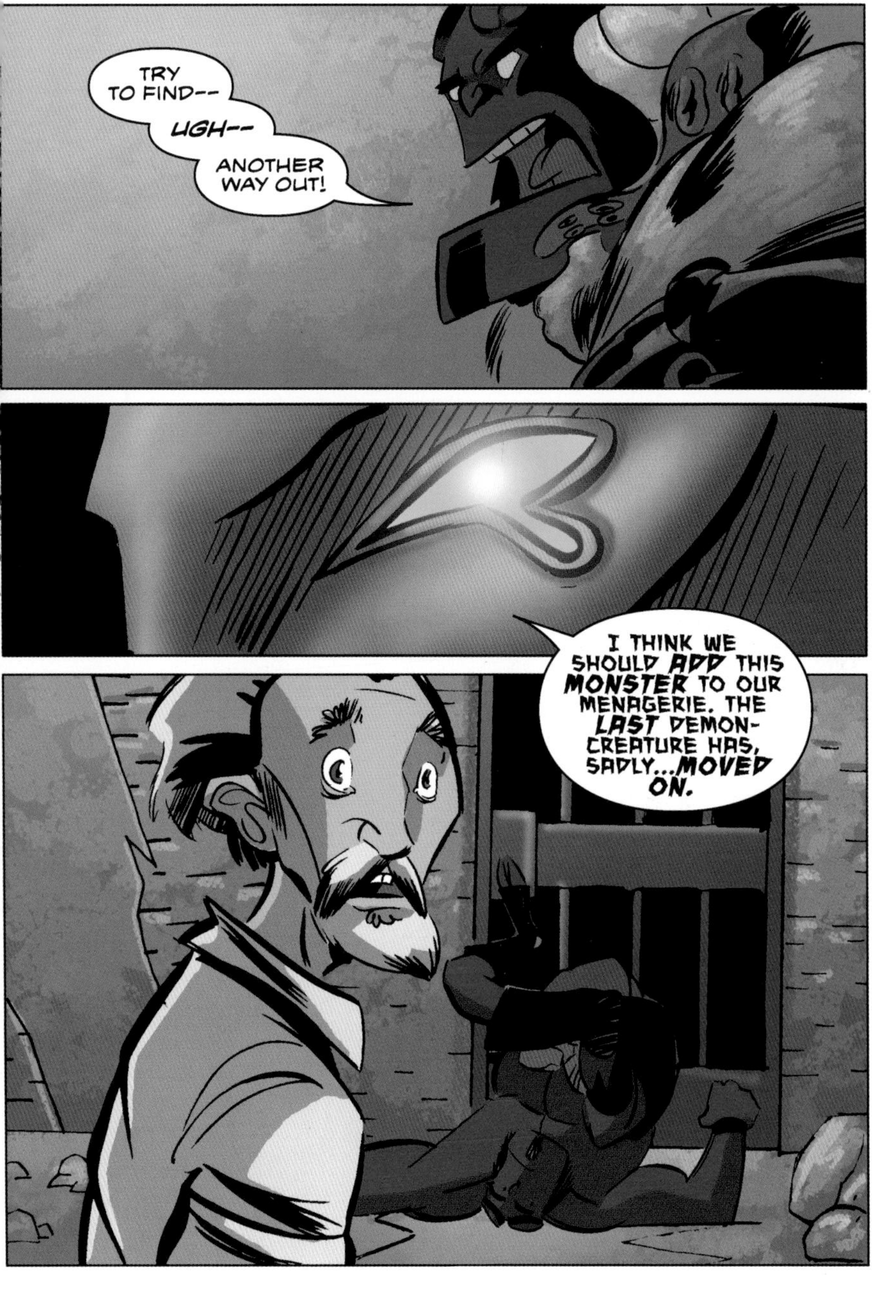
TRY TO FIND--
UGH--
ANOTHER WAY OUT!
I THINK WE SHOULD ADD THIS MONSTER TO OUR MENAGERIE. THE LAST DEMON-CREATURE HAS, SADLY...MOVED ON.

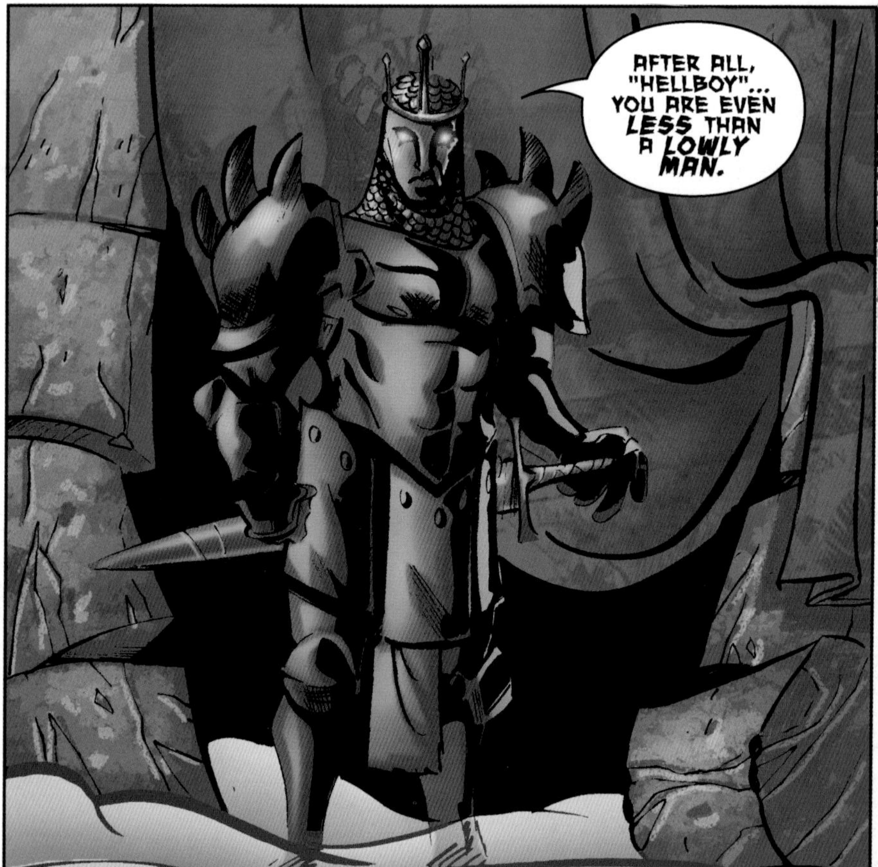
AFTER ALL, "HELLBOY"... YOU ARE EVEN LESS THAN A LOWLY MAN.

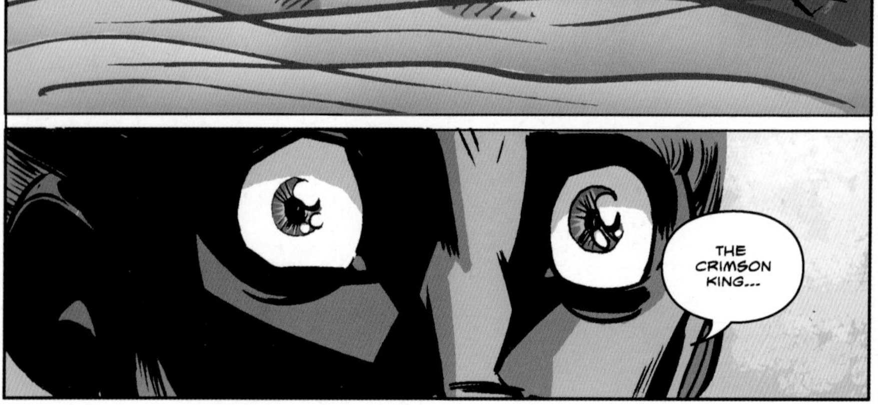
THE CRIMSON KING...

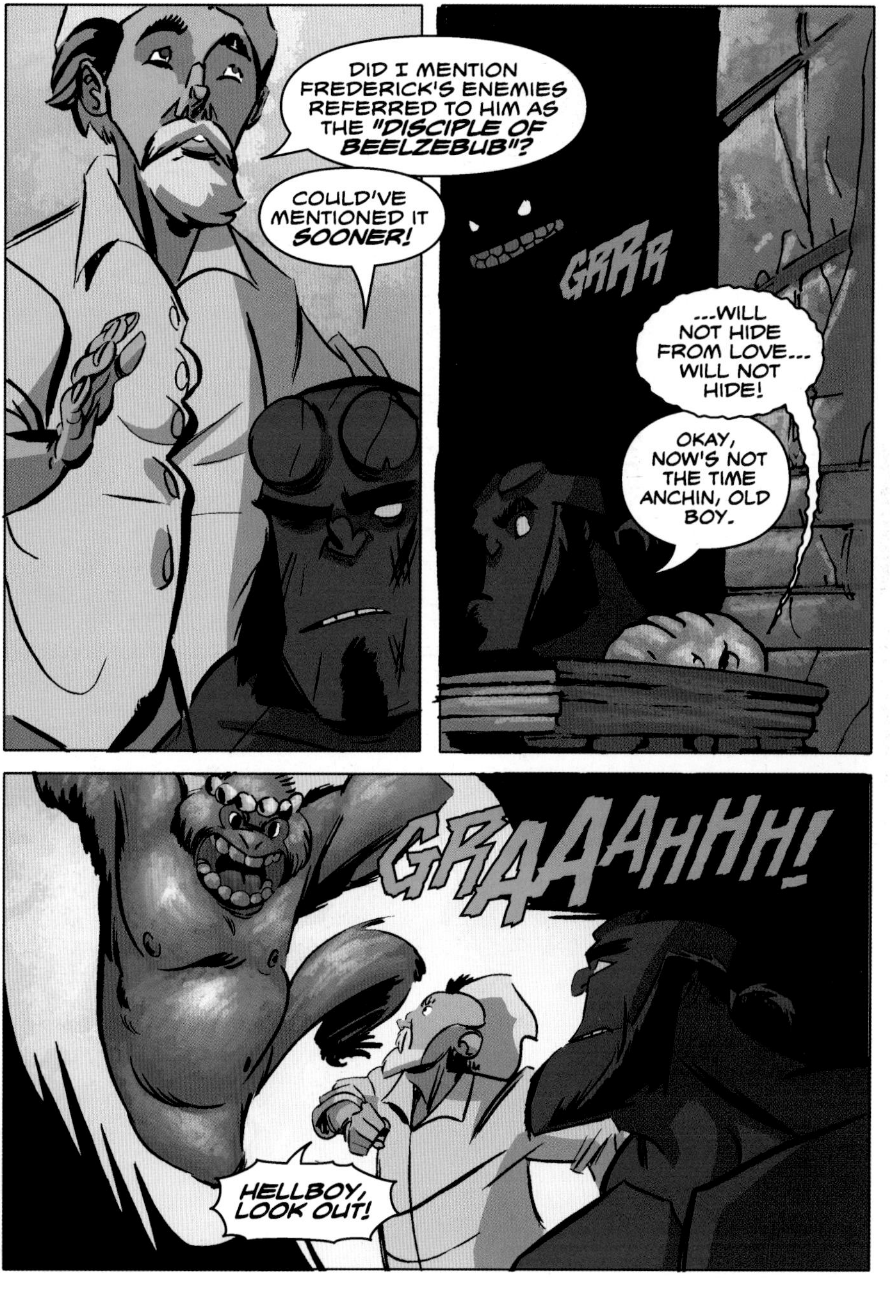
DID I MENTION FREDERICK'S ENEMIES REFERRED TO HIM AS THE "DISCIPLE OF BEELZEBUB"?
COULD'VE MENTIONED IT SOONER!
GRRR
...WILL NOT HIDE FROM LOVE... WILL NOT HIDE!
OKAY, NOW'S NOT THE TIME ANCHIN, OLD BOY.
GRAAAHHH!
HELLBOY, LOOK OUT!

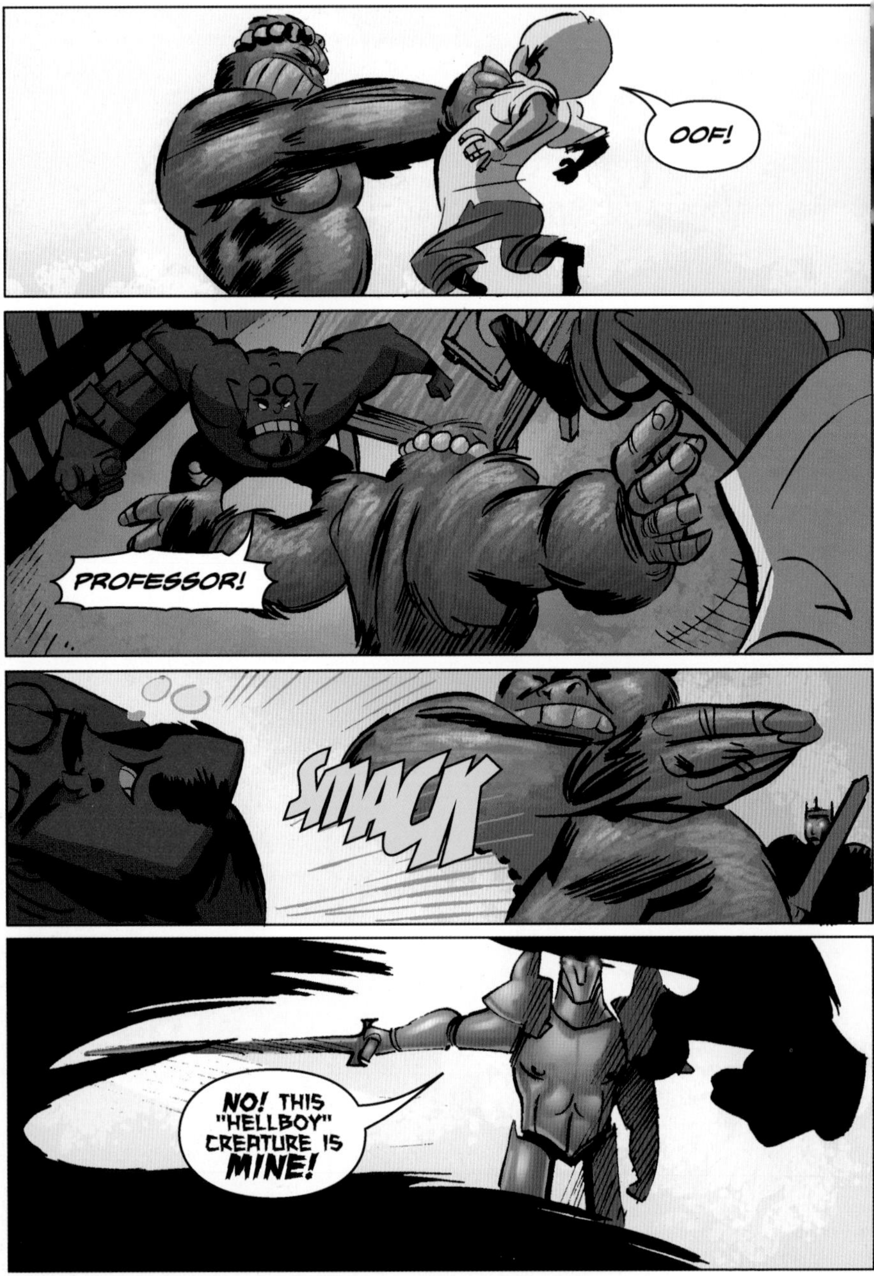
OOF!
PROFESSOR!
SMACK
NO! THIS "HELLBOY" CREATURE IS MINE!

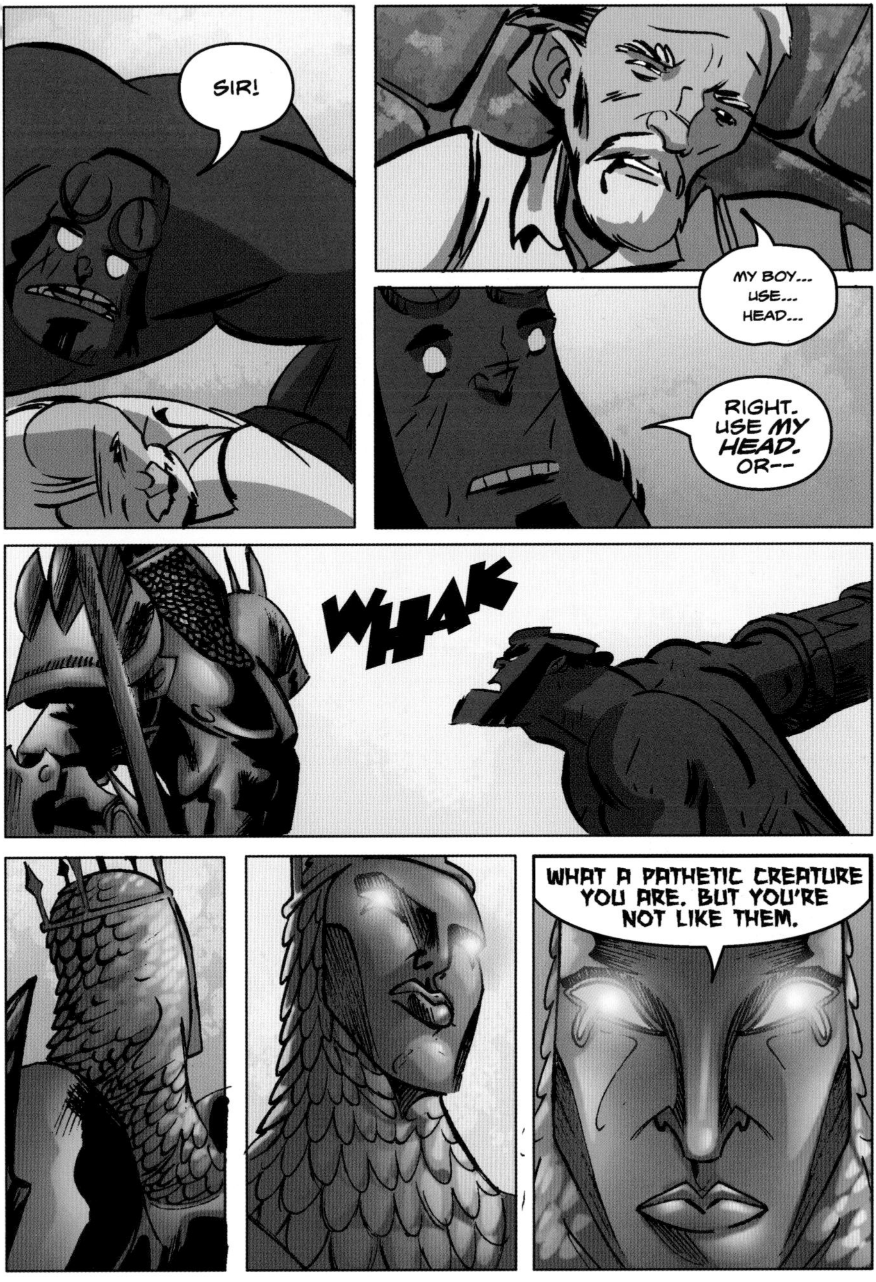
SIR!
MY BOY... USE... HEAD...
RIGHT. USE MY HEAD. OR--
WHAK
WHAT A PATHETIC CREATURE YOU ARE. BUT YOU'RE NOT LIKE THEM.

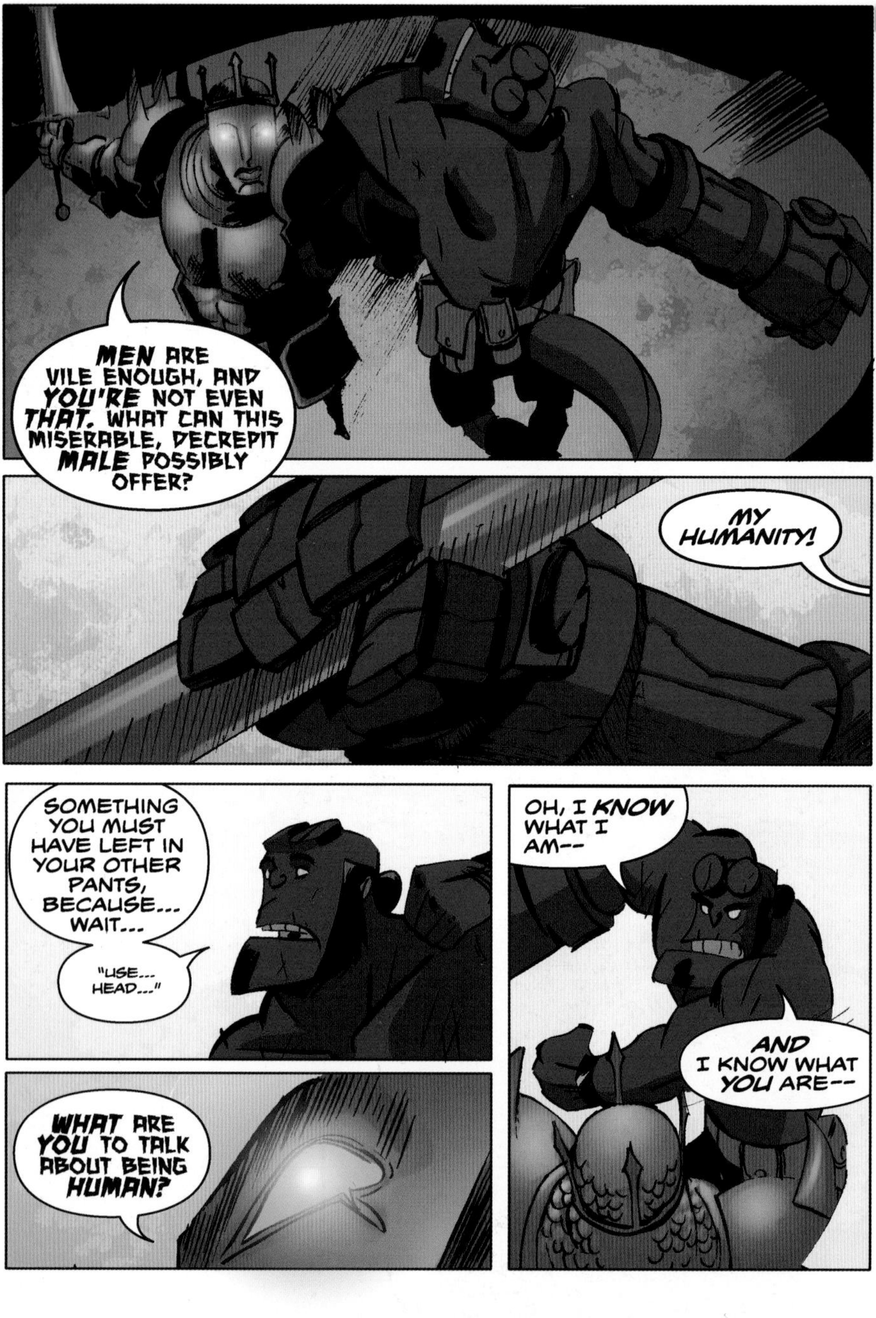
MEN ARE VILE ENOUGH, AND YOU'RE NOT EVEN THAT. WHAT CAN THIS MISERABLE, DECREPIT MALE POSSIBLY OFFER?
MY HUMANITY!
SOMETHING YOU MUST HAVE LEFT IN YOUR OTHER PANTS, BECAUSE... WAIT...
"USE... HEAD..."
WHAT ARE YOU TO TALK ABOUT BEING HUMAN?
OH, I KNOW WHAT I AM--
AND I KNOW WHAT YOU ARE--

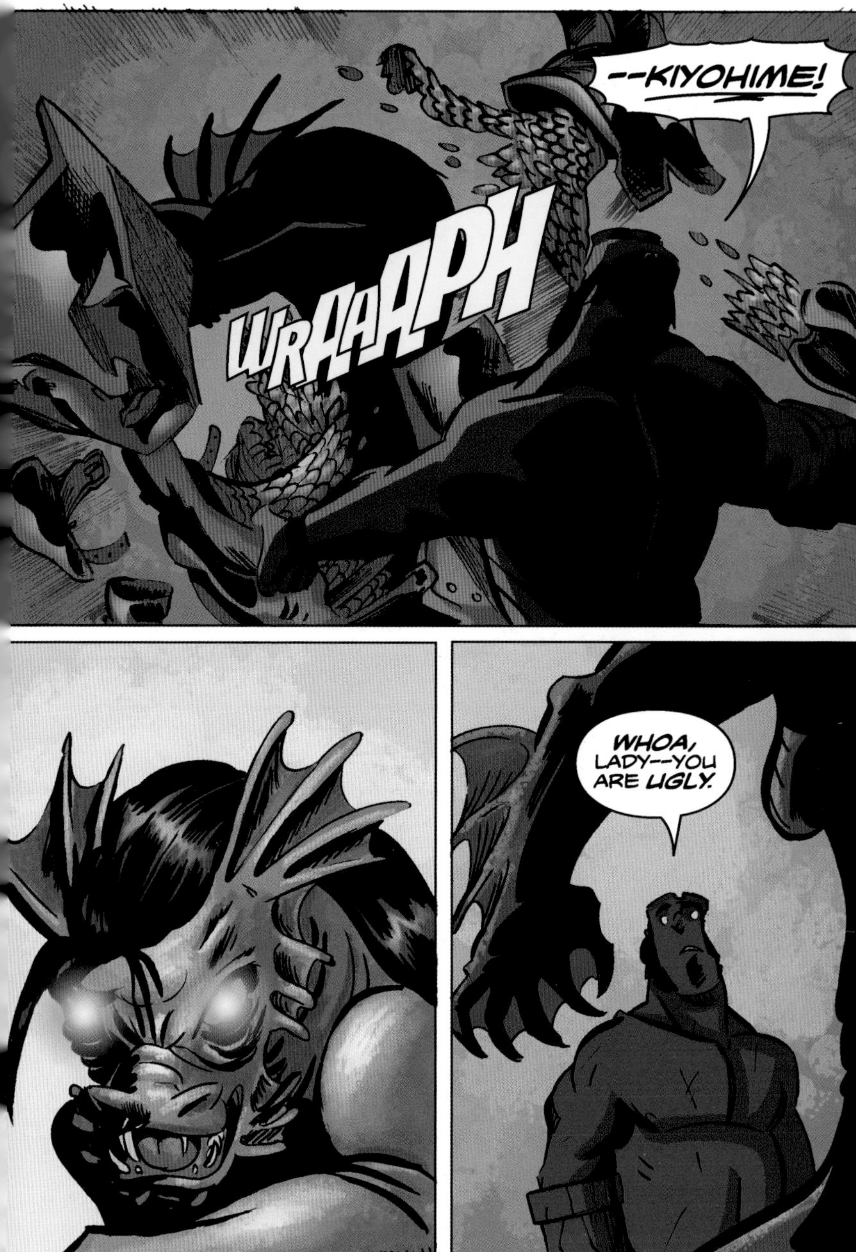
--KIYOHIME!
WRAAAAPH
WHOA, LADY--YOU ARE UGLY.

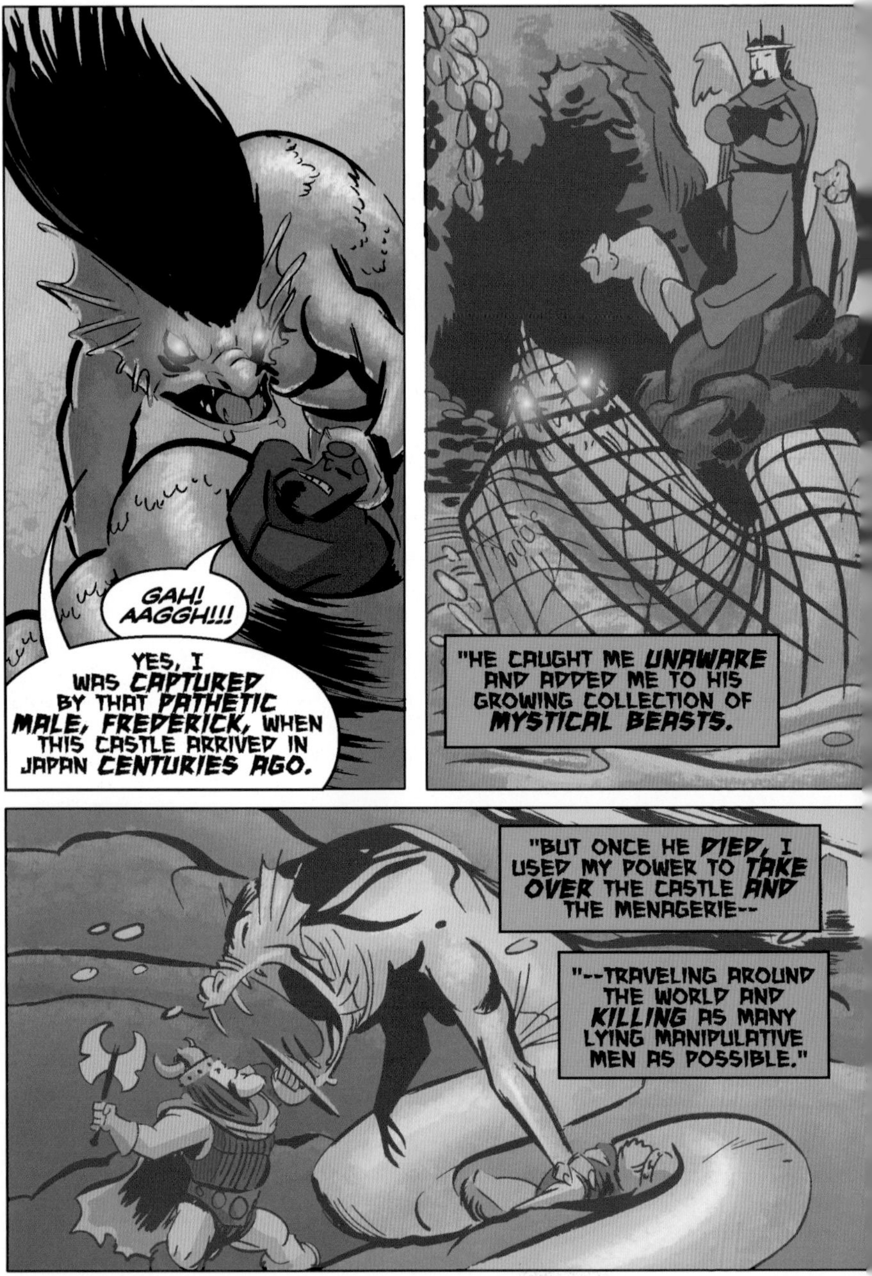
GAH! AAGGH!!!
YES, I WAS CAPTURED BY THAT PATHETIC MALE, FREDERICK, WHEN THIS CASTLE ARRIVED IN JAPAN CENTURIES AGO.
"HE CAUGHT ME UNAWARE AND ADDED ME TO HIS GROWING COLLECTION OF MYSTICAL BEASTS.
"BUT ONCE HE DIED, I USED MY POWER TO TAKE OVER THE CASTLE AND THE MENAGERIE--
"--TRAVELING AROUND THE WORLD AND KILLING AS MANY LYING MANIPULATIVE MEN AS POSSIBLE."

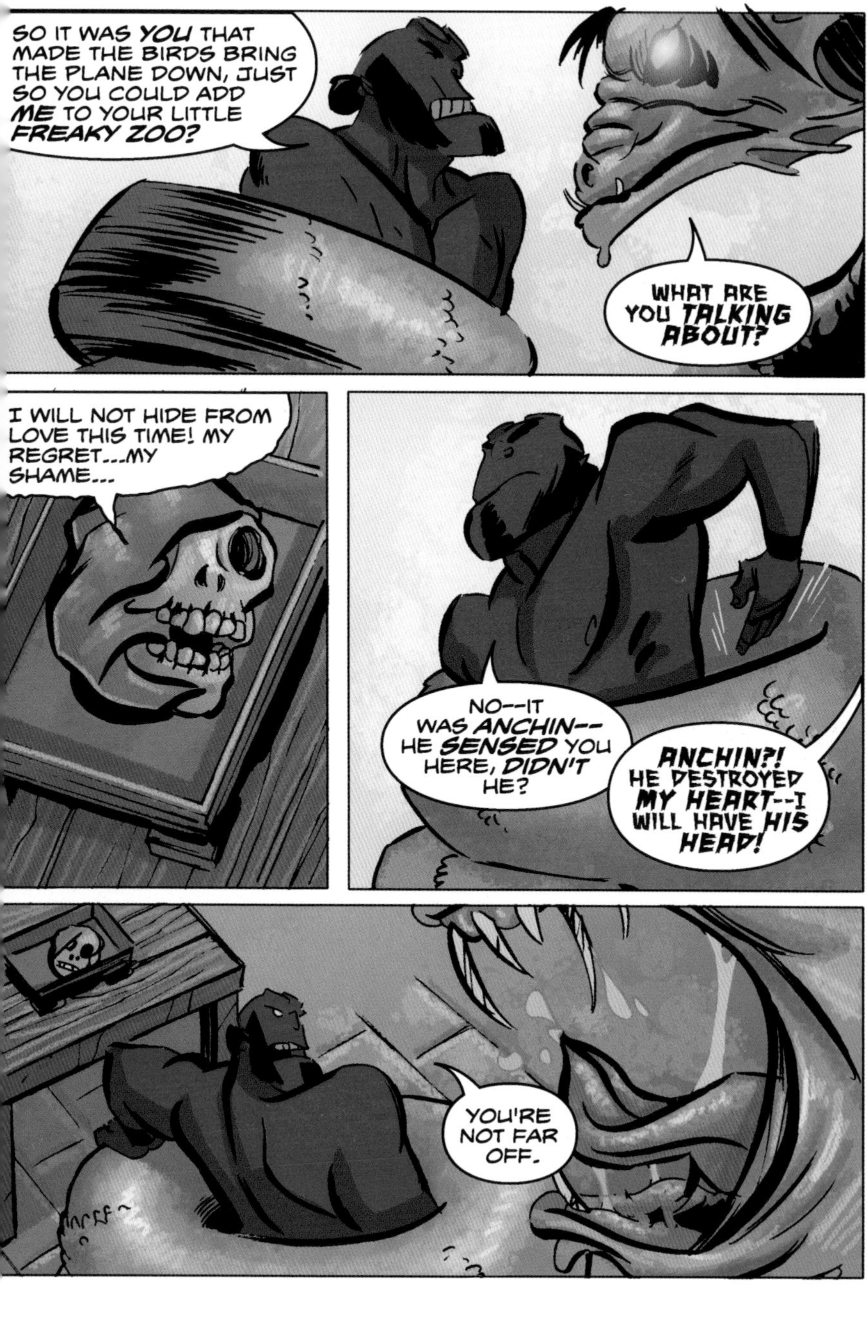
SO IT WAS YOU THAT MADE THE BIRDS BRING THE PLANE DOWN, JUST SO YOU COULD ADD ME TO YOUR LITTLE FREAKY ZOO?
WHAT ARE YOU TALKING ABOUT?
I WILL NOT HIDE FROM LOVE THIS TIME! MY REGRET...MY SHAME...
NO--IT WAS ANCHIN--HE SENSED YOU HERE, DIDN'T HE?
ANCHIN?! HE DESTROYED MY HEART--I WILL HAVE HIS HEAD!
YOU'RE NOT FAR OFF.

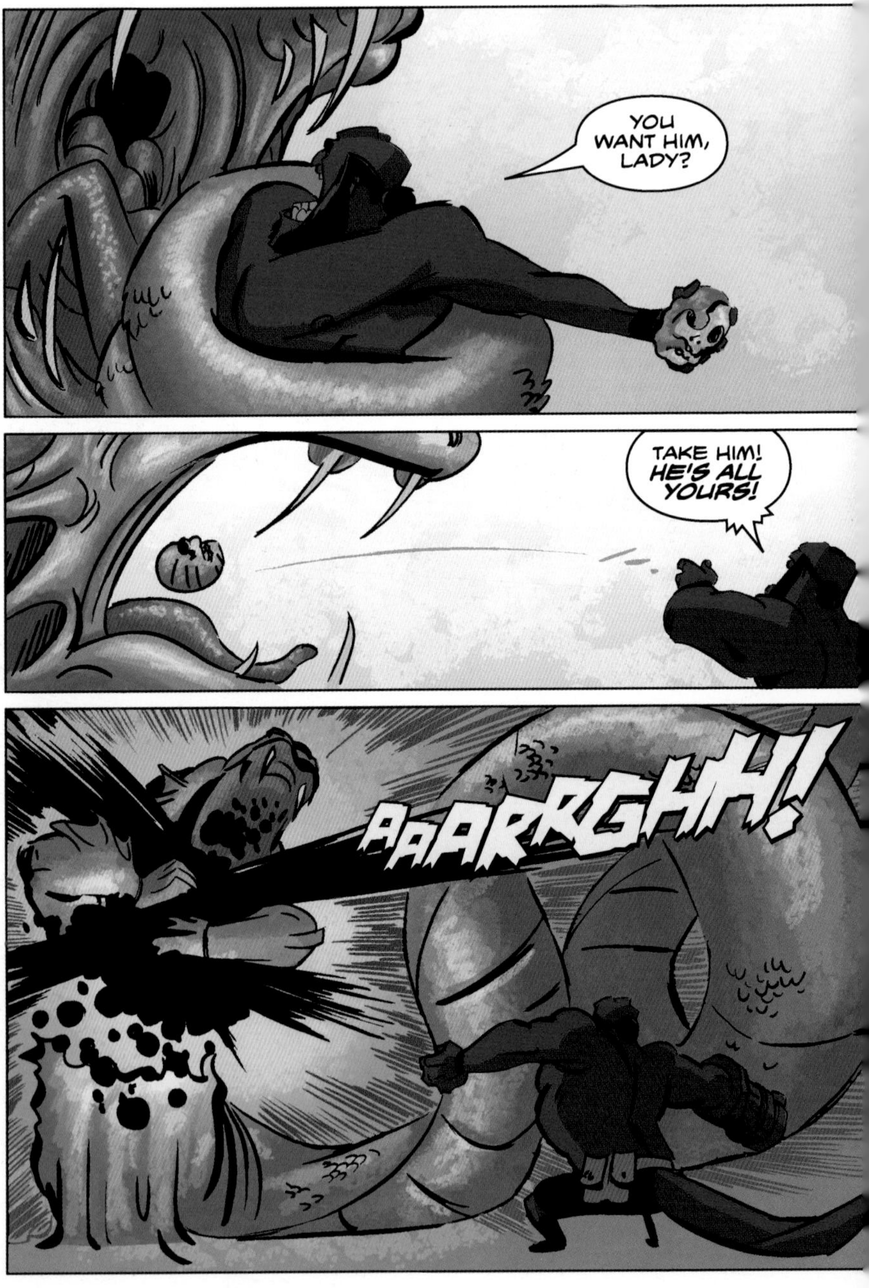
YOU WANT HIM, LADY?
TAKE HIM! HE'S ALL YOURS!
AAARRGHH!

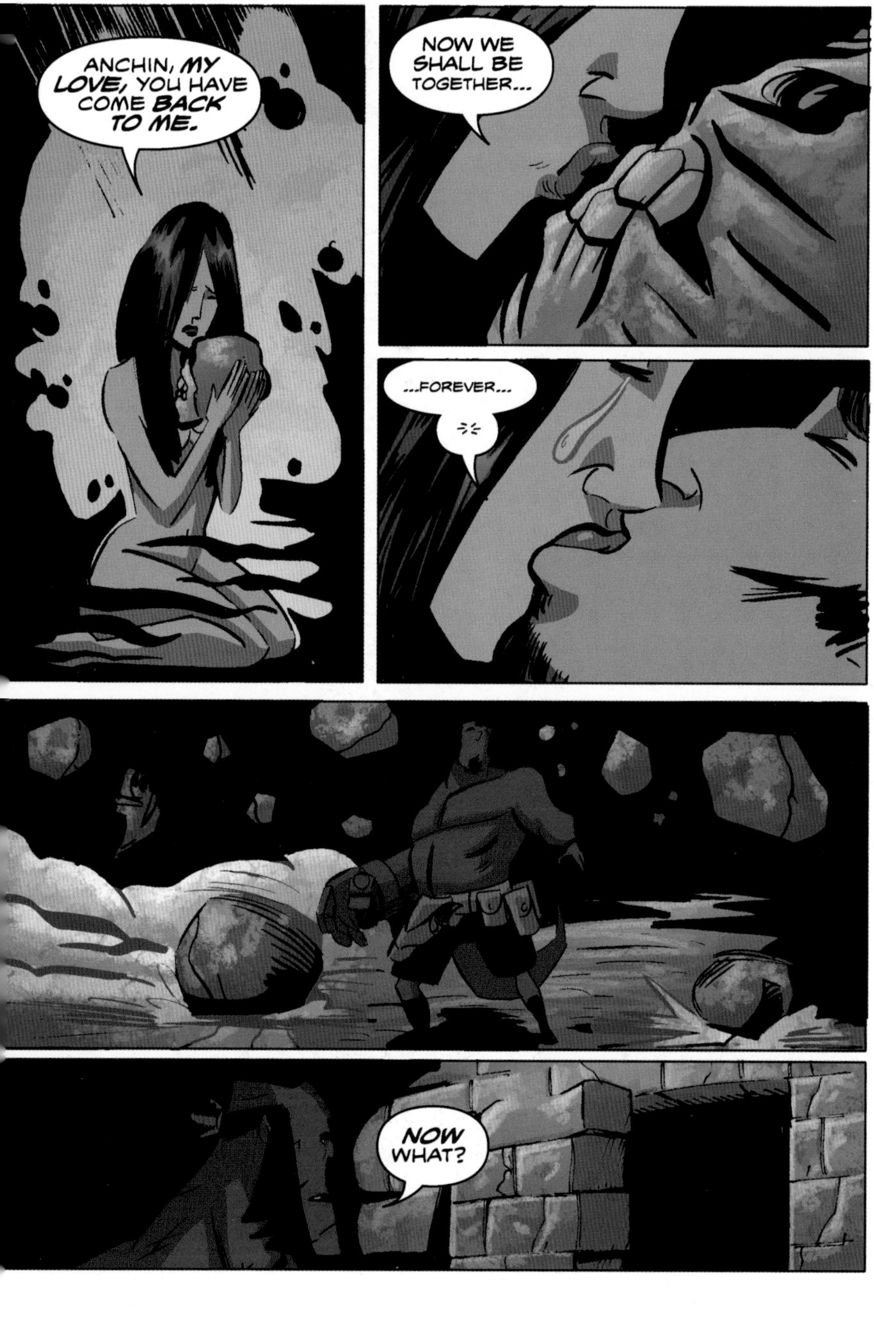
ANCHIN, MY LOVE, YOU HAVE COME BACK TO ME.
NOW WE SHALL BE TOGETHER...
...FOREVER...
NOW WHAT?

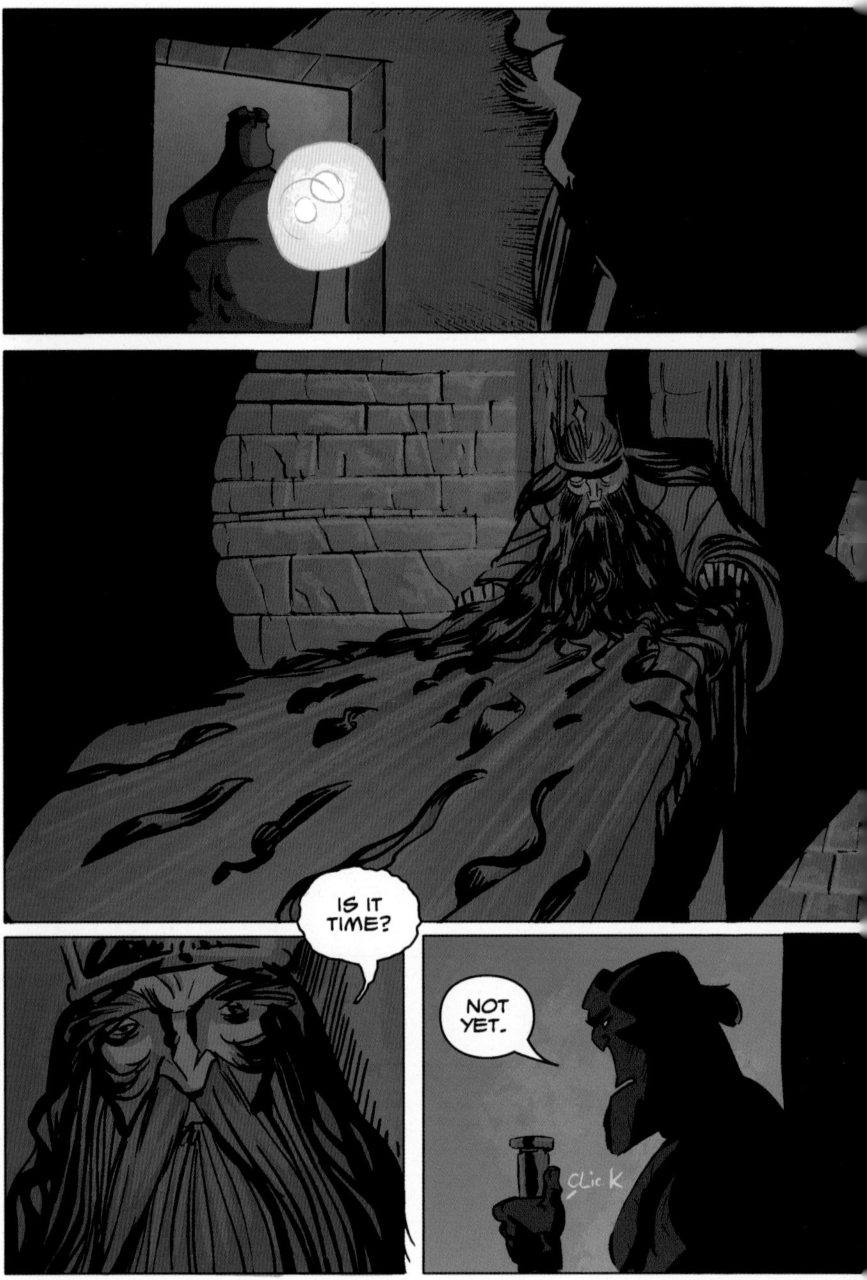
IS IT TIME?
NOT YET.
CLICK

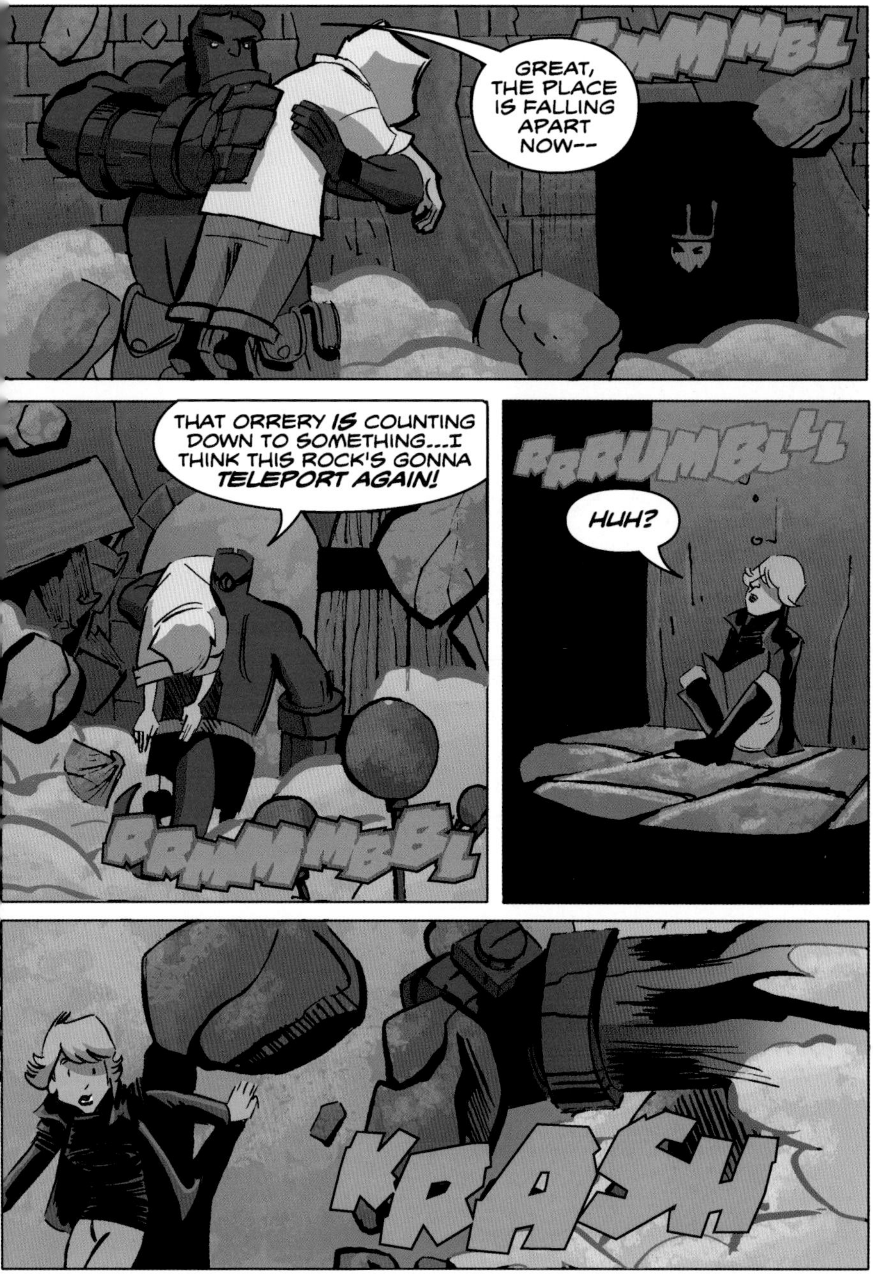
RMMMBL
GREAT, THE PLACE IS FALLING APART NOW--
THAT ORRERY IS COUNTING DOWN TO SOMETHING...I THINK THIS ROCK'S GONNA TELEPORT AGAIN!
RRMMMMBBL
RRRUMBLLL
HUH?
KRASH

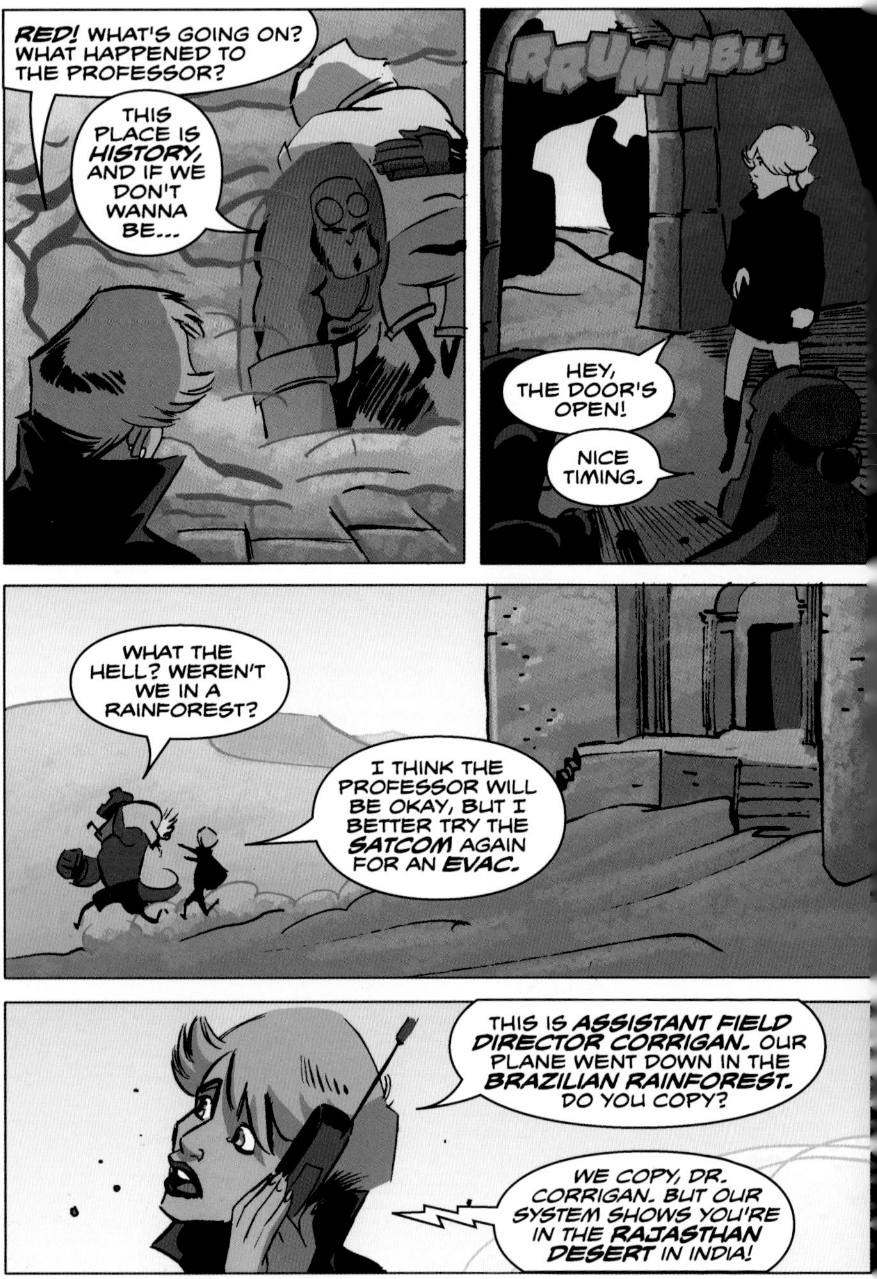
RED! WHAT'S GOING ON? WHAT HAPPENED TO THE PROFESSOR?
THIS PLACE IS HISTORY, AND IF WE DON'T WANNA BE...
RRUMMBLL
HEY, THE DOOR'S OPEN!
NICE TIMING.
WHAT THE HELL? WEREN'T WE IN A RAINFOREST?
I THINK THE PROFESSOR WILL BE OKAY, BUT I BETTER TRY THE SATCOM AGAIN FOR AN EVAC.
THIS IS ASSISTANT FIELD DIRECTOR CORRIGAN. OUR PLANE WENT DOWN IN THE BRAZILIAN RAINFOREST. DO YOU COPY?
WE COPY, DR. CORRIGAN. BUT OUR SYSTEM SHOWS YOU'RE IN THE RAJASTHAN DESERT IN INDIA!

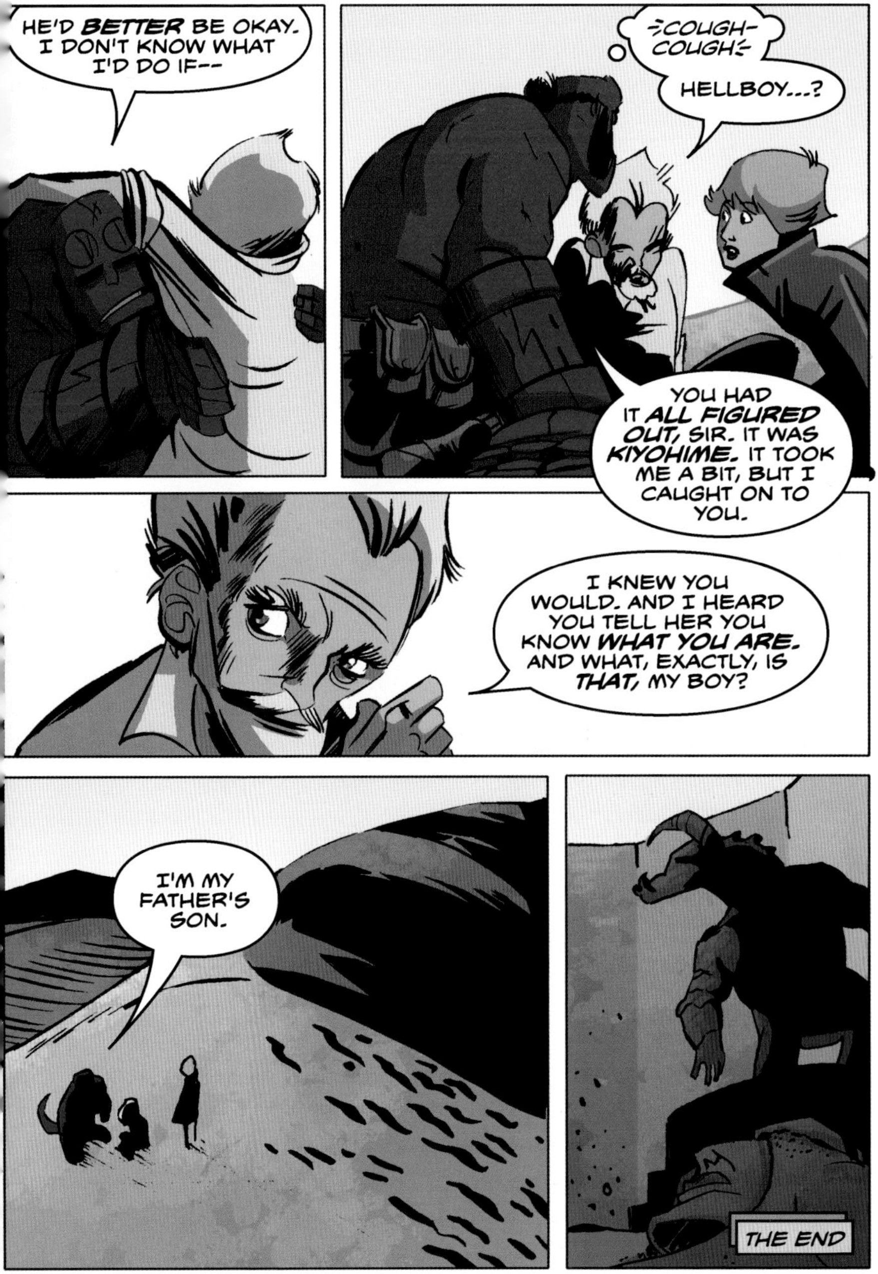
HE'D BETTER BE OKAY. I DON'T KNOW WHAT I'D DO IF--
≈COUGH- COUGH≈
HELLBOY...?
YOU HAD IT ALL FIGURED OUT, SIR. IT WAS KIYOHIME. IT TOOK ME A BIT, BUT I CAUGHT ON TO YOU.
I KNEW YOU WOULD. AND I HEARD YOU TELL HER YOU KNOW WHAT YOU ARE. AND WHAT, EXACTLY, IS THAT, MY BOY?
I'M MY FATHER'S SON.
THE END

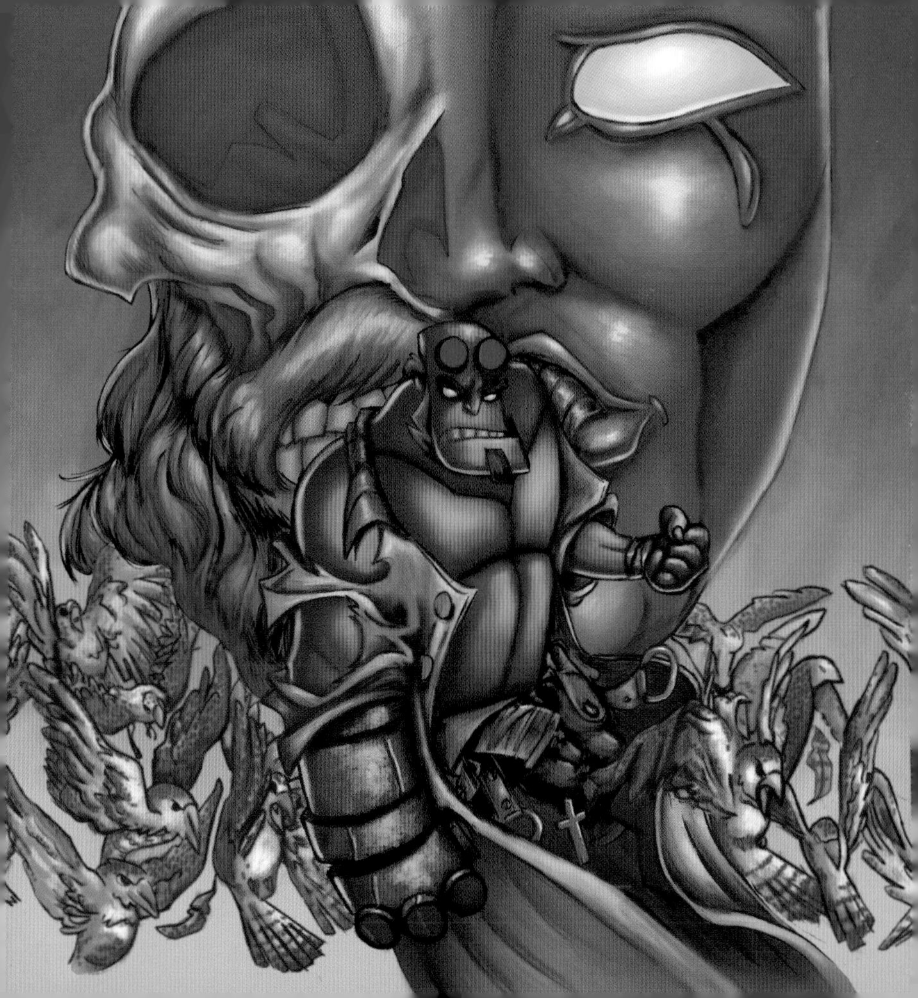

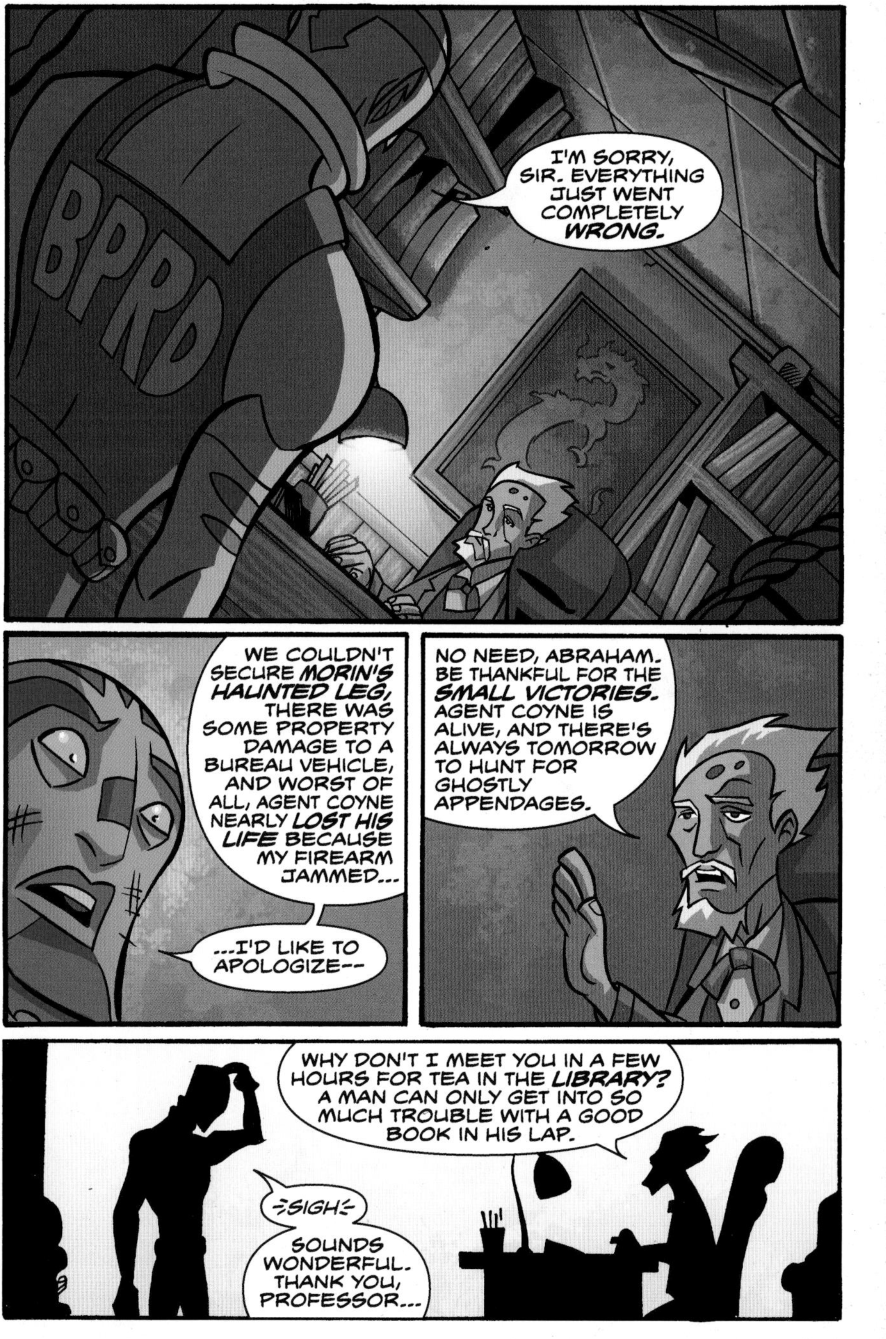
I'M SORRY, SIR. EVERYTHING JUST WENT COMPLETELY WRONG.
WE COULDN'T SECURE MORIN'S HAUNTED LEG, THERE WAS SOME PROPERTY DAMAGE TO A BUREAU VEHICLE, AND WORST OF ALL, AGENT COYNE NEARLY LOST HIS LIFE BECAUSE MY FIREARM JAMMED...
...I'D LIKE TO APOLOGIZE--
NO NEED, ABRAHAM. BE THANKFUL FOR THE SMALL VICTORIES. AGENT COYNE IS ALIVE, AND THERE'S ALWAYS TOMORROW TO HUNT FOR GHOSTLY APPENDAGES.
WHY DON'T I MEET YOU IN A FEW HOURS FOR TEA IN THE LIBRARY? A MAN CAN ONLY GET INTO SO MUCH TROUBLE WITH A GOOD BOOK IN HIS LAP.
SIGH
SOUNDS WONDERFUL. THANK YOU, PROFESSOR...

SMALL VICTORIES

ZZZ

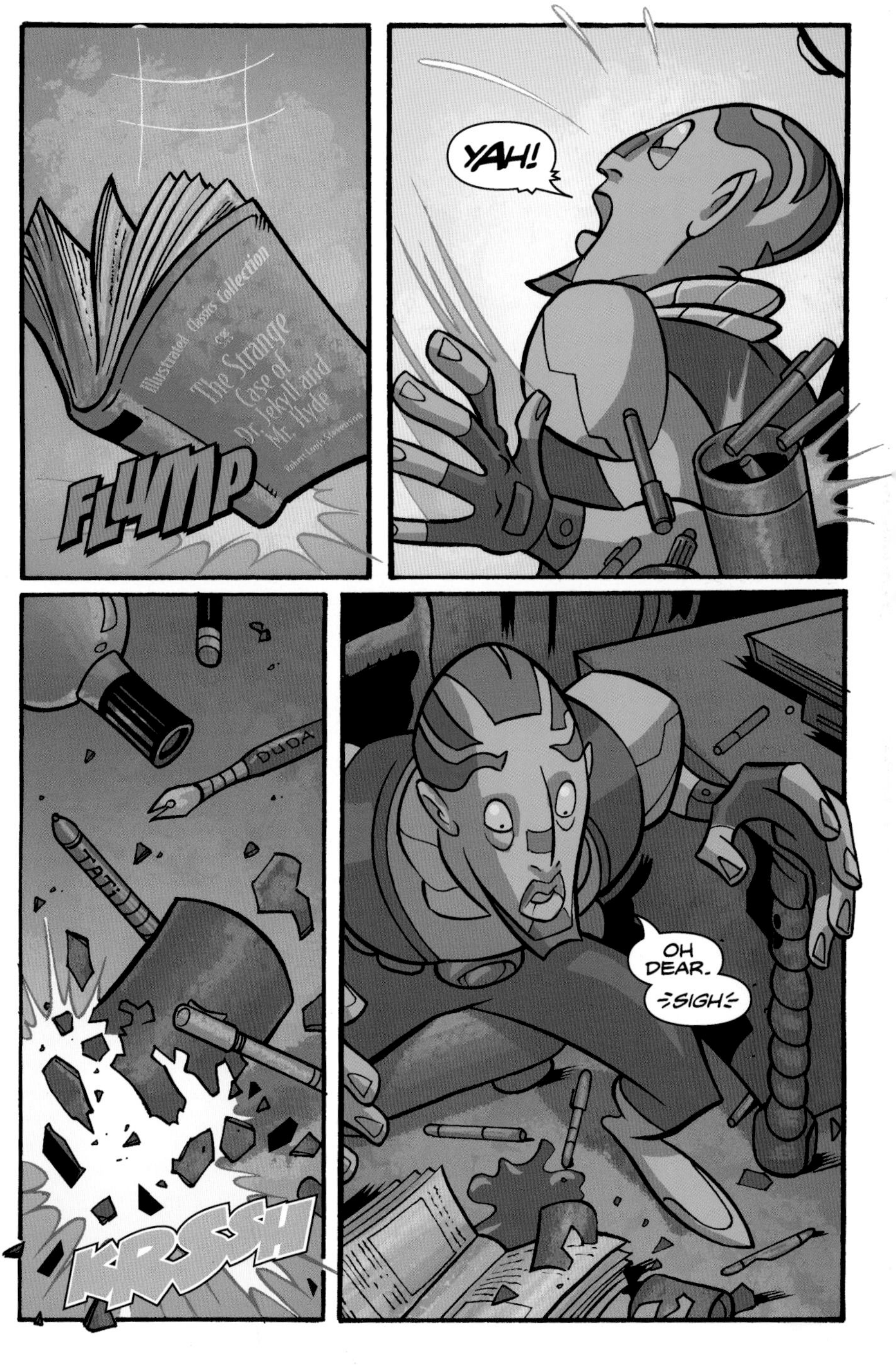
Illustrated Classics Collection
The Strange Case of Dr. Jekyll and Mr. Hyde
Robert Louis Stevenson
FLUMP
YAH!
DUDA
TATI
KRSSH
OH DEAR.
SIGH

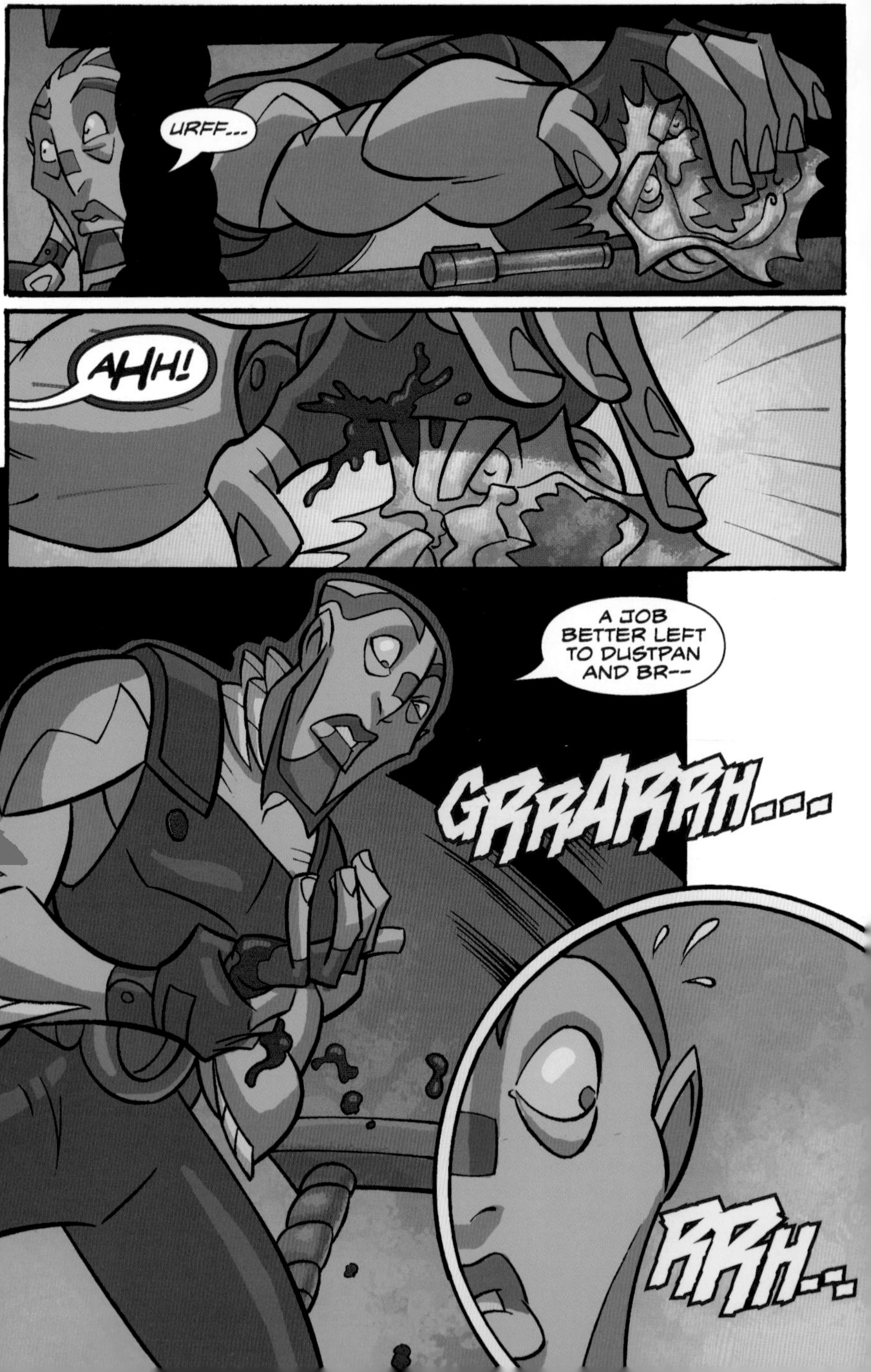
URFF...
AHH!
A JOB BETTER LEFT TO DUSTPAN AND BR--
GRRARRH....
RRH..

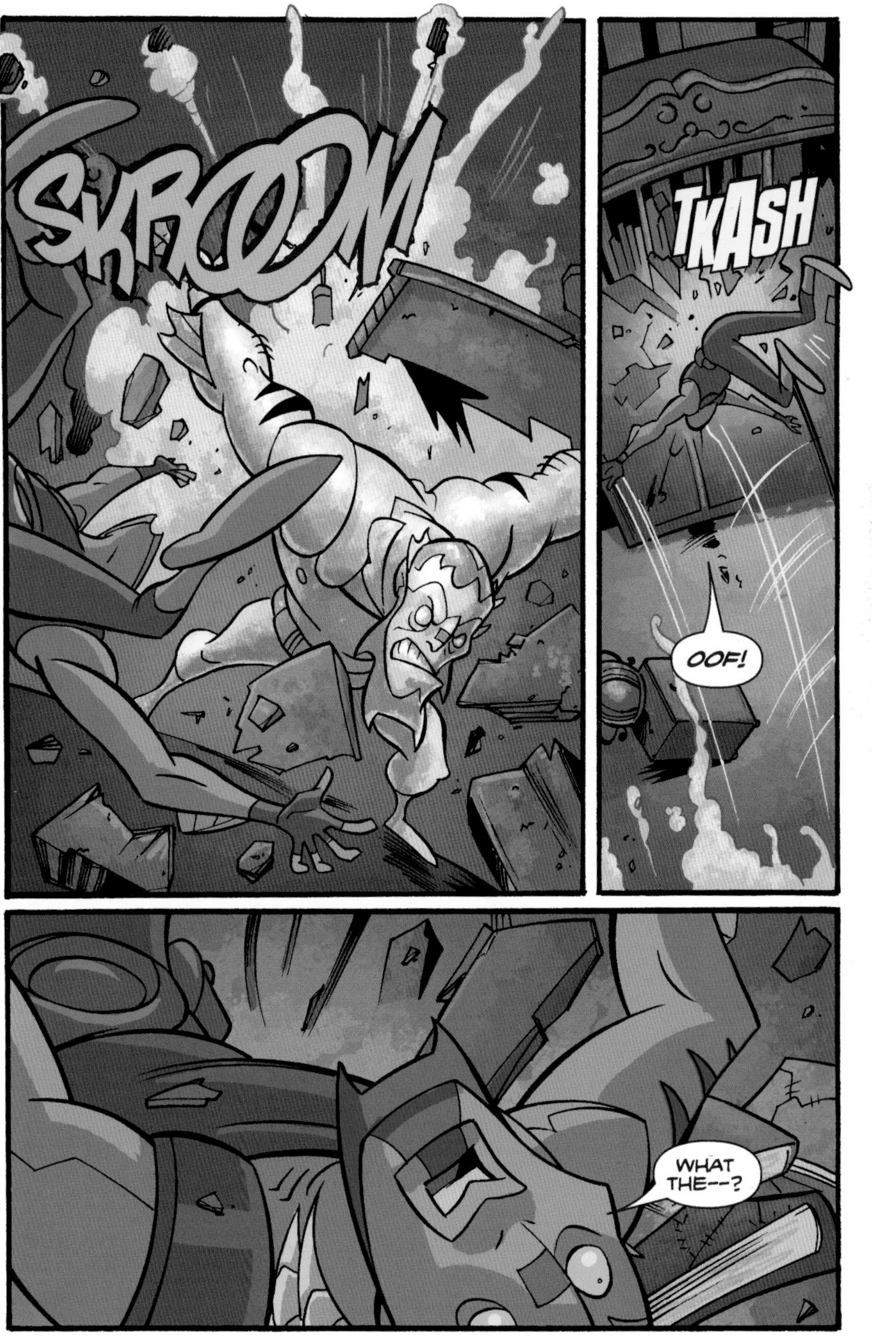
SKROOM
TKASH
OOF!
WHAT THE--?

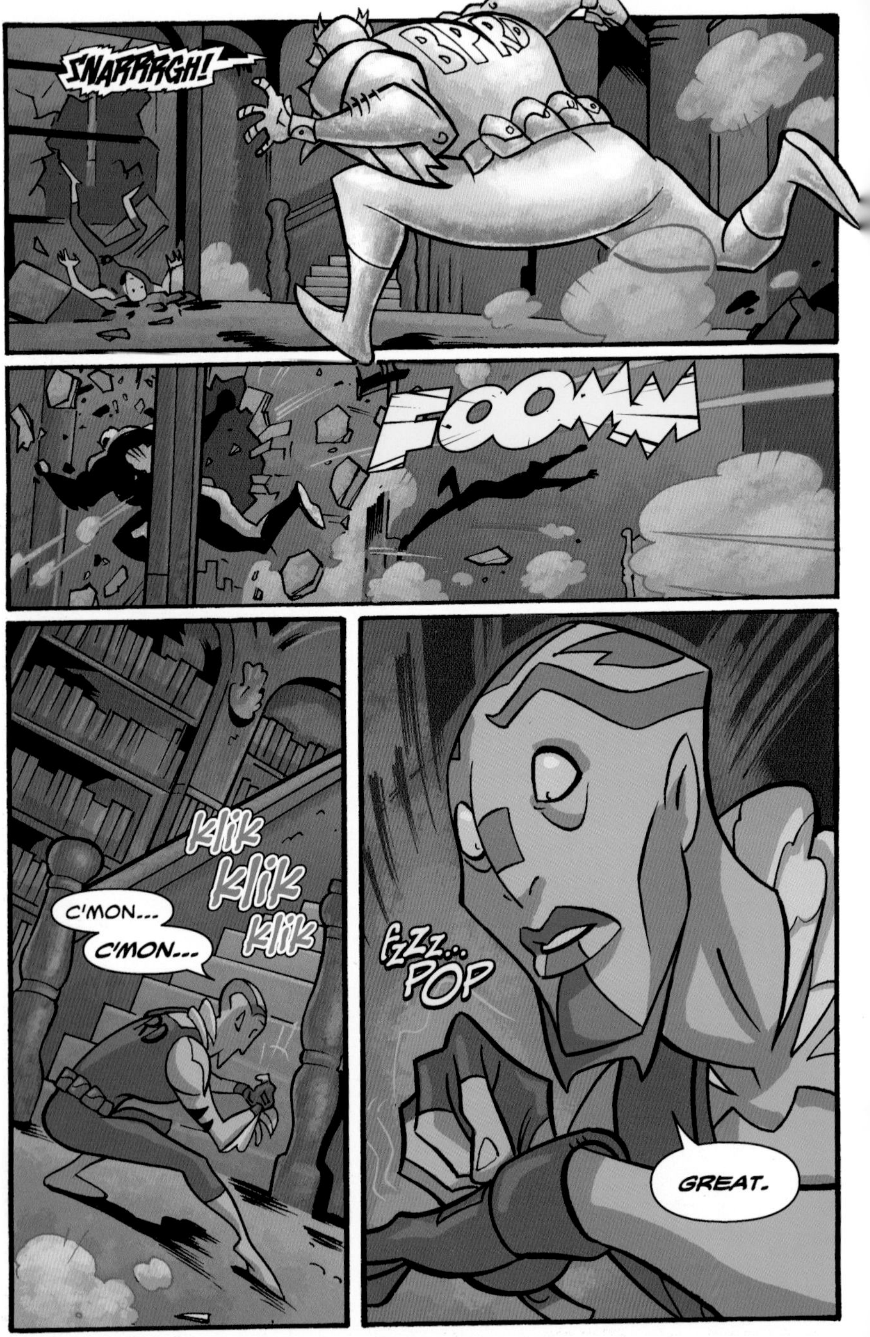
SNARRRGH!
FOOM
klik
klik
klik
C'MON...
C'MON...
fzzz... POP
GREAT.

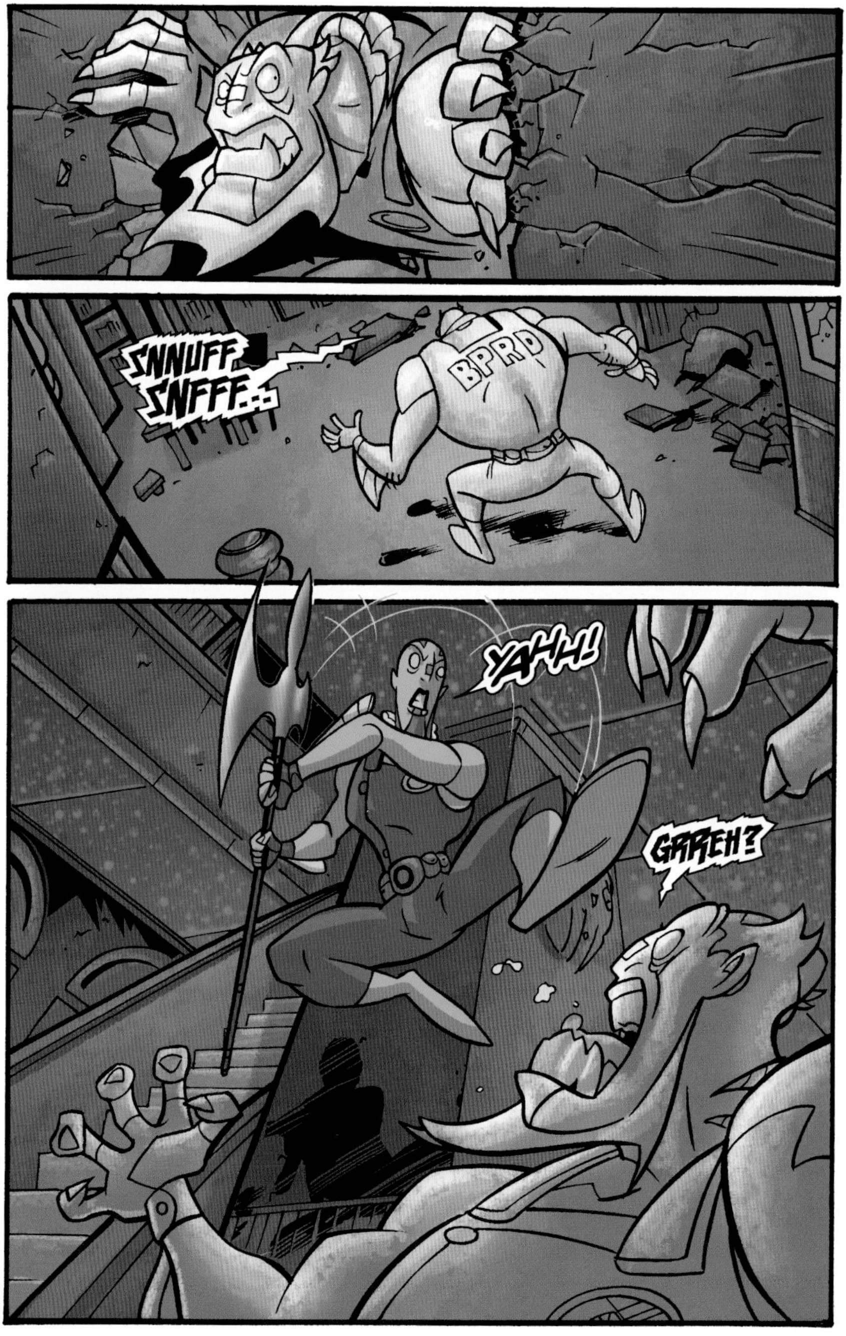
SNNUFF SNFFF...
BPRD
YAHH!
GRREH?

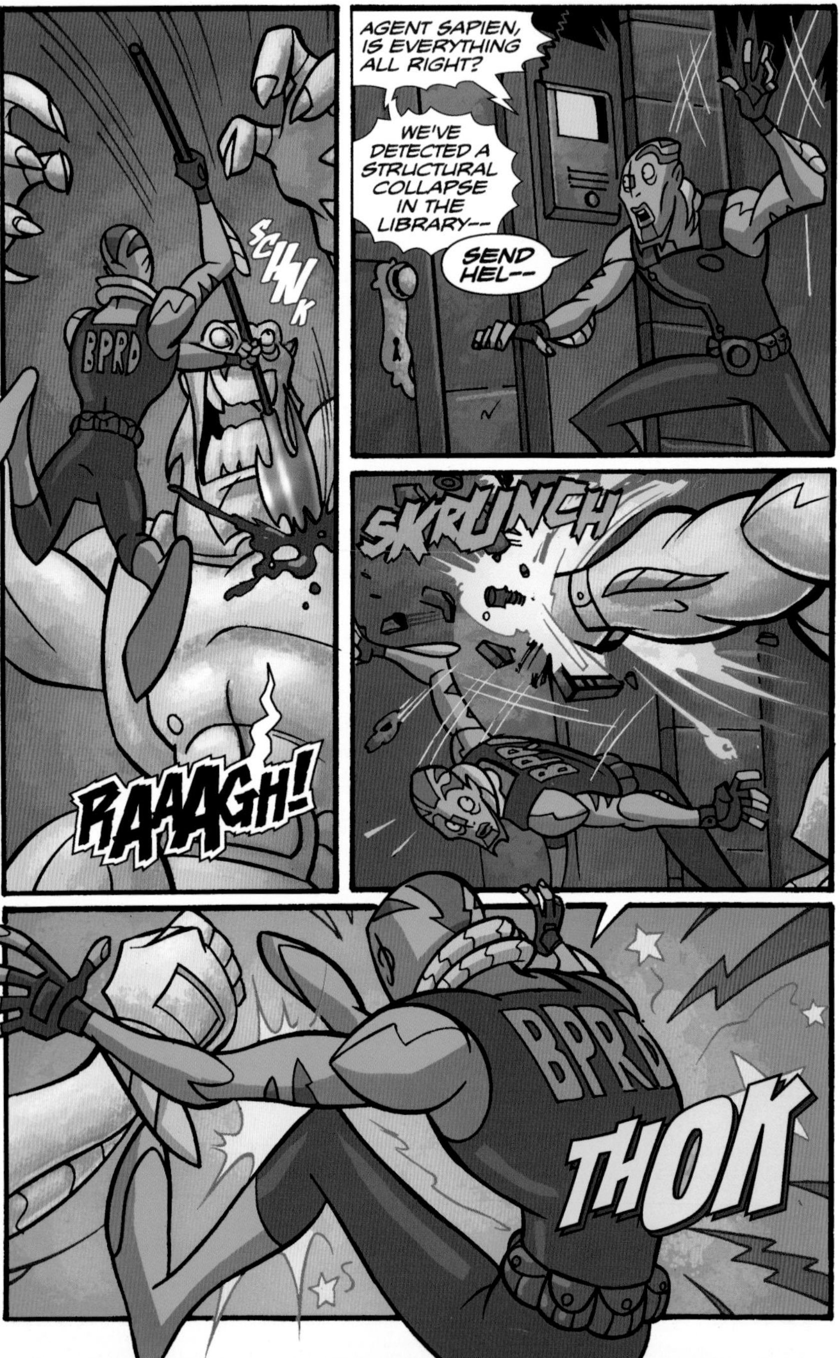
SCHNK
RAAAGH!
AGENT SAPIEN, IS EVERYTHING ALL RIGHT?
WE'VE DETECTED A STRUCTURAL COLLAPSE IN THE LIBRARY--
SEND HEL--
SKRUNCH
THOK

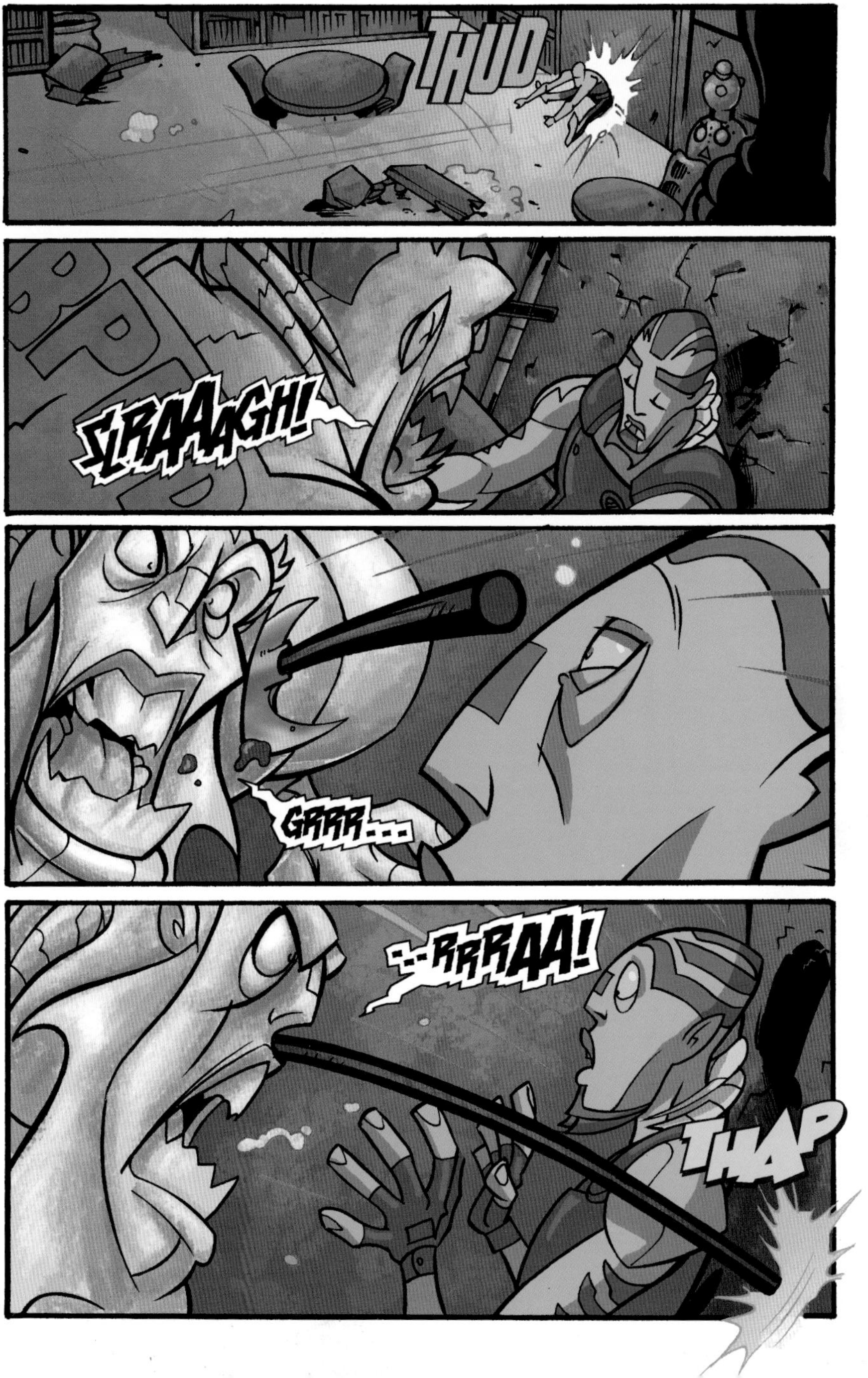
THUD
SCRAAAGH!
GRRR...
...RRRAA!
THAP

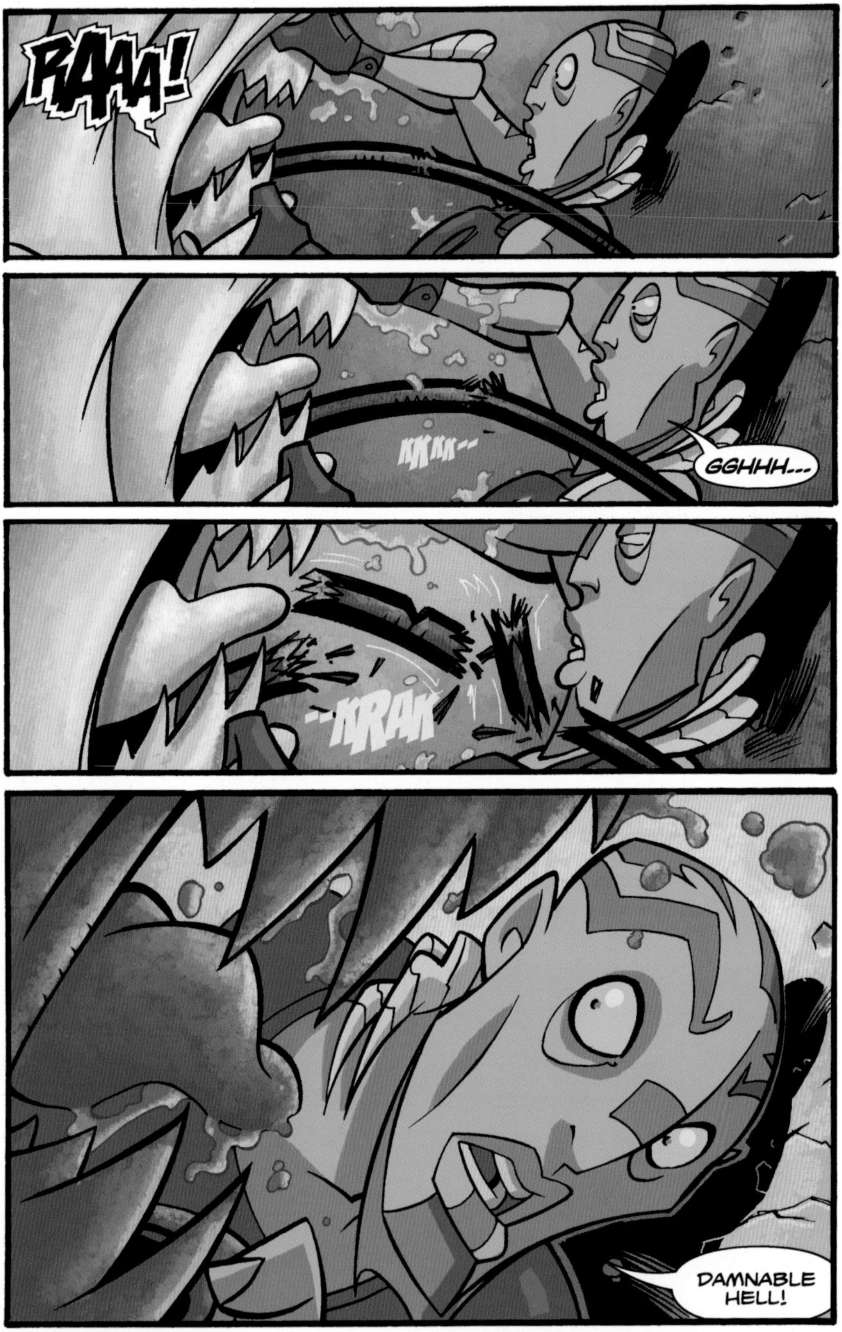
RAAA!
KKKK--
GGHHH...
--KRAK
DAMNABLE HELL!

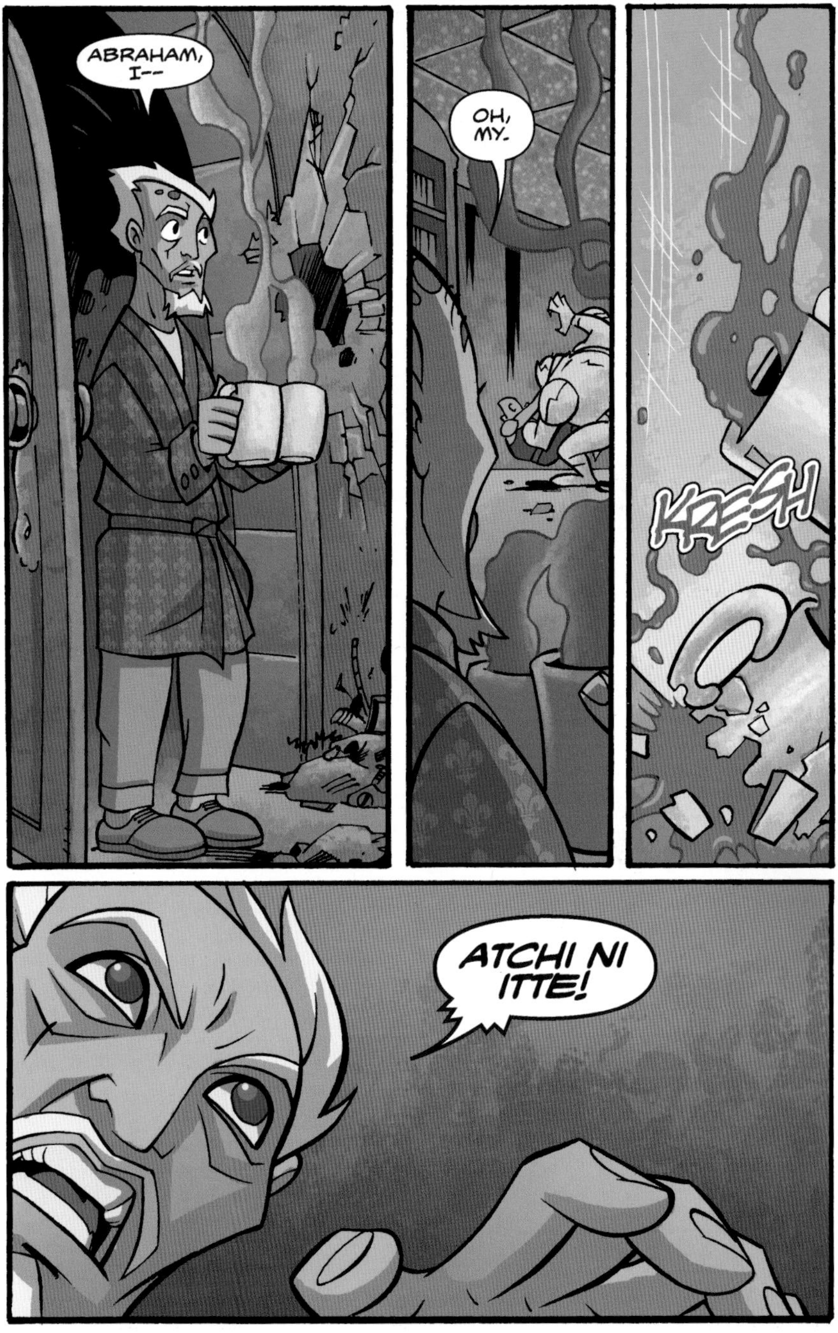
ABRAHAM, I--
OH, MY.
KRESH
ATCHI NI ITTE!

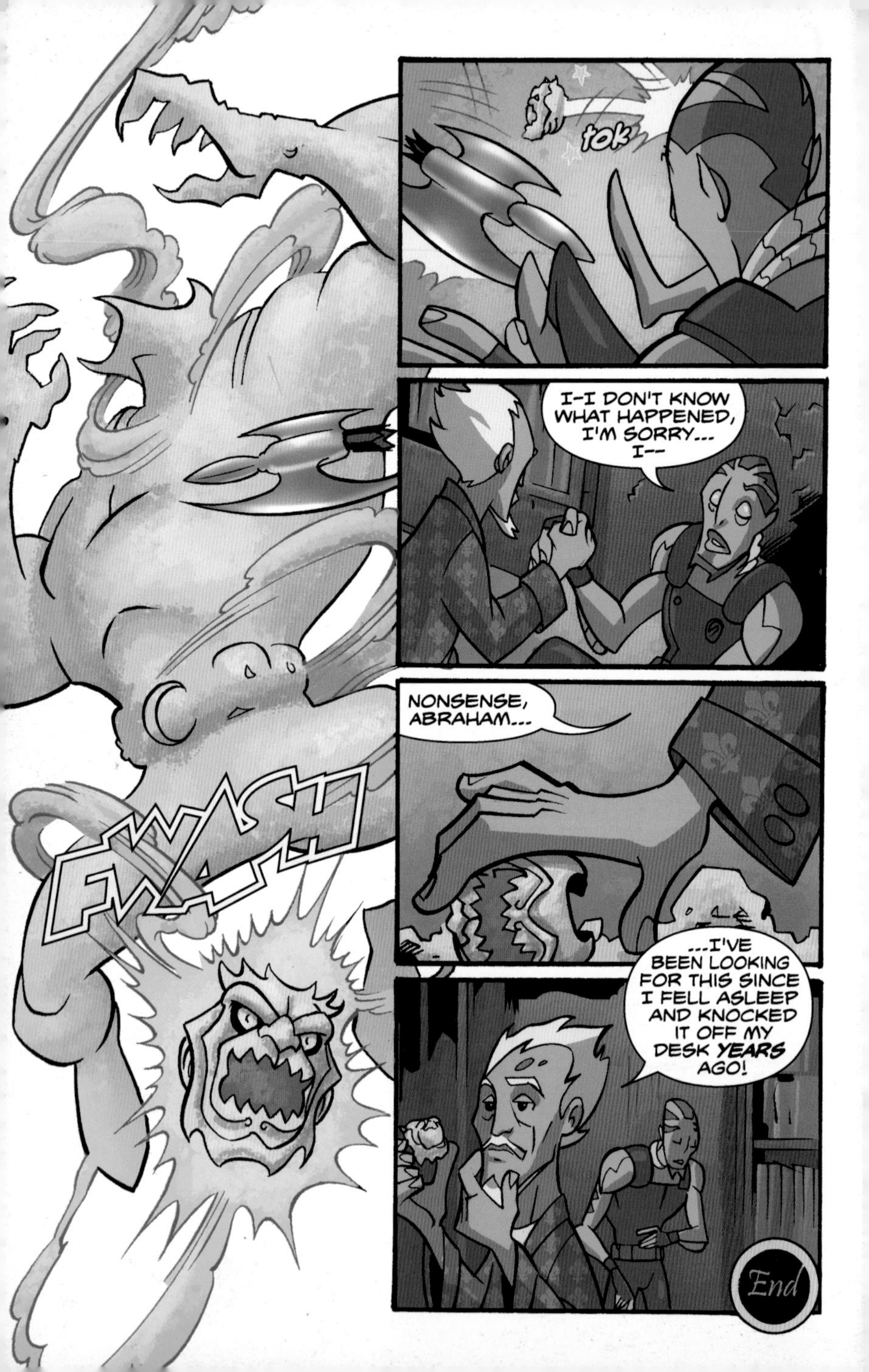
FWASH
tok
I-I DON'T KNOW WHAT HAPPENED, I'M SORRY... I--
NONSENSE, ABRAHAM...
...I'VE BEEN LOOKING FOR THIS SINCE I FELL ASLEEP AND KNOCKED IT OFF MY DESK YEARS AGO!
End

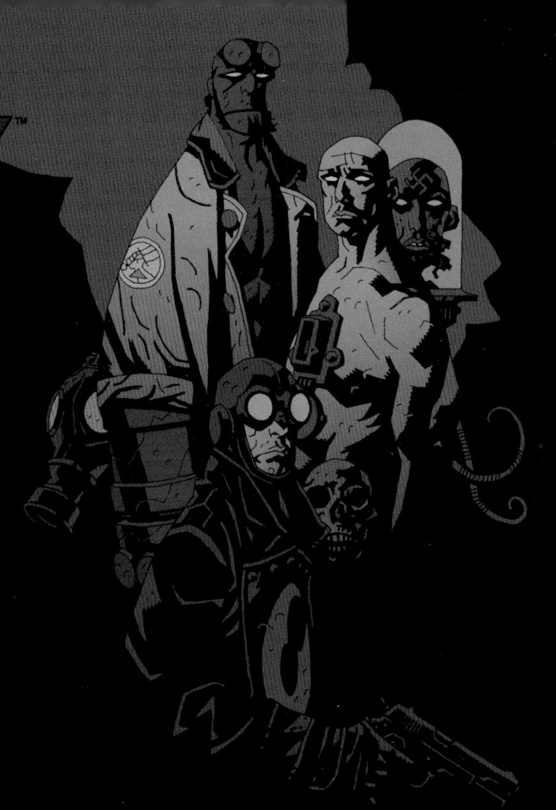

HELLBOY™

by MIKE MIGNOLA

SEED OF DESTRUCTION
with John Byrne
ISBN-10: 1-59307-094-2
ISBN-13: 978-1-59307-094-6
$17.95

WAKE THE DEVIL
ISBN-10: 1-59307-095-0
ISBN-13: 978-1-59307-095-3
$17.95

THE CHAINED COFFIN
AND OTHERS
ISBN-10: 1-59307-091-8
ISBN-13: 978-1-59307-091-5
$17.95

THE RIGHT HAND OF DOOM
ISBN-10: 1-59307-093-4
ISBN-13: 978-1-59307-093-9
$17.95

CONQUEROR WORM
ISBN-10: 1-59307-092-6
ISBN-13: 978-1-59307-092-2
$17.95

STRANGE PLACES
ISBN-10: 1-59307-475-1
ISBN-13: 978-1-59307-475-3
$17.95

THE ART OF HELLBOY
ISBN-10: 1-59307-089-6
ISBN-13: 978-1-59307-089-2
$29.95

B.P.R.D.: HOLLOW EARTH
By Mignola, Chris Golden,
Ryan Sook and others
ISBN-10: 1-56971-862-8
ISBN-13: 978-1-56971-862-9
$17.95

B.P.R.D.: THE SOUL OF VENICE
By Mignola, Mike Oeming, Guy
Davis, Scott Kolins, Geoff Johns
and others
ISBN-10: 1-59307-132-9
ISBN-13: 978-1-59307-132-5
$17.95

B.P.R.D.: PLAGUE OF FROGS
By Mignola and Guy Davis
ISBN-10: 1-59307-288-0
ISBN-13: 978-1-59307-288-9
$17.95

B.P.R.D.: THE DEAD
By Mignola, John Arcudi and
Guy Davis
ISBN-10: 1-59307-380-1
ISBN-13: 978-1-59307-380-0
$17.95

B.P.R.D.: THE BLACK FLAME
By Mignola, Arcudi and Davis
ISBN-10: 1-59307-550-2
ISBN-13: 978-1-59307-550-7
$17.95

B.P.R.D.:
THE UNIVERSAL MACHINE
By Mignola, Arcudi and Davis
ISBN-10: 1-59307-710-6
ISBN-13: 978-1-59307-710-5
$17.95

To find a comics shop in your area,
call 1-888-266-4226.
For more information or to order direct:
• On the web: darkhorse.com
• Email: mailorder@darkhorse.com
• Phone: 1-800-862-0052
Mon.-Fri. 9 A.M. to 5 P.M. Pacific Time.

DARK HORSE COMICS™ drawing on your nightmares
darkhorse.com

DARK HORSE

darkhorse.com | DARK HORSE TWENTY YEARS

COMICS | BOOKS | PRODUCTS | REVIEWS | ZONES | NEWS | HELP | COMPANY | RESOURCES

VISIT THE HELLBOY™ ZONE ON DARKHORSE.COM TO EXPLORE GREAT FEATURES LIKE:

- Exclusive content from editors on upcoming projects!
- Exclusive downloadable desktops!
- Online previews and animations!
- Message Boards!
- Up-to-date information on the latest releases!
- Links to other cool Hellboy sites.

Visit DARKHORSE.COM/HELLBOY for more details!

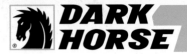

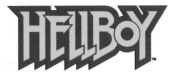

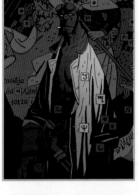

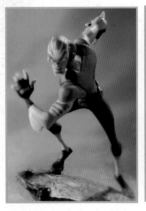

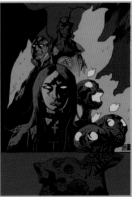

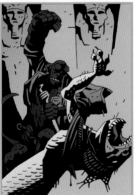